Cuba

by Richard Sale

Richard Sale took up writing full time
after spending many years as a research
scientist. He has contributed to a
number of magazines, chiefly on outdoor
topics; of the 25 or so books he
has had published, most are travel
guides to European destinations,
including *Essential Ibiza & Formentera* in
this series.
Richard lives on the Cotswold Way in
Gloucestershire.

Above: an array of Cuban dolls in national dress

AA Publishing

Above: *a typical* guajiro
(farmer)

Written by Richard Sale
First published 1998
Reprinted October 1999
Revised second edition 2000
Reprinted Aug 2002
Reprinted 2004. Information verified and updated.
Reprinted Feb 2005.
Reprinted Oct 2006

Published by AA Publishing, a trading name of Automobile
Association Developments Limited, whose registered
office is Fanum House, Basing View, Basingstoke,
Hampshire RG21 4EA. Registered number 1878835.

Find out more about
AA Publishing and the
wide range of travel
publications and services
the AA provides by
visiting our website at
www.theAA.com/travel

A03211

Colour separation: Pace Colour, Southampton
Printed and bound in Italy by Printer Trento S.r.l.

Contents

About this Book

This book is divided into five sections to cover the most important aspects of your visit to Cuba.

Viewing Cuba pages 5–14
An introduction to Cuba by the author.
Features of Cuba
Essence of Cuba
The Shaping of Cuba
Peace and Quiet
Cuba's Famous

Top Ten pages 15–26
The author's choice of the Top Ten places to see in Cuba, listed in alphabetical order, each with practical information.

What to See pages 27–100
The four main areas of Cuba, each with its own brief introduction and an alphabetical listing of the main attractions.
Practical information
Snippets of 'Did You Know…' information
4 suggested walks
4 suggested tours
2 features

Where To... pages 101–116
Detailed listings of the best places to eat, stay, shop, take the children and be entertained.

Practical Matters pages 117–24
A highly visual section containing essential travel information.

Maps
All map references are to the individual maps found in the What to See section of this guide.
For example, Guantánamo has the reference ✚ 29F1 – indicating the page on which the map is located and the grid square in which the town is to be found. A list of the maps that have been used in this travel guide can be found in the index.
A good, large-scale map is essential when going on a drive in Cuba. The signing of roads and turnings is erratic and cannot always be relied upon.

Prices
Where appropriate, an indication of the cost of an establishment is given by £ signs:
£££ denotes higher prices, ££ denotes average prices, while £ denotes lower charges.

Star Ratings
Most of the places described in this book have been given a separate rating:
❂❂❂ Do not miss
❂❂ Highly recommended
❂ Worth seeing

4

Viewing
Cuba

Above: *Palm trees and classic cars on Playas del Este*

Richard Sale's Cuba

Say it Right

As with travelling anywhere, learning a few words of the local language is an effort that will be well rewarded. In Cuba it is best to start with the name of the country itself. To the Cubans it is 'Koo-ba', not 'Queue-ba' as English speakers tend to say. The capital is La Habana – pronounced La Ab-anna – the city folk being Habaneros, the 'h' again being dropped.

Cuba lies just 150km from the Florida shore of the mainland USA, and is a mere island hop away from Jamaica, but the island's isolation following the revolution of late 1958 meant that for a long time few visitors ever reached it. Now, as Cuba expands its tourist trade in its quest for much-needed foreign currency, the island is open again and everyone can enjoy the delights of one of the most alluring islands in the Caribbean.

Flying into Havana from Europe, the visitor is usually treated to a superb view of Cuba's northern coast. The waters of the Atlantic – all shades from turquoise to a rich, deep blue – come as no surprise, but the marvellous tapestry of greens that forms the countryside, from the light green of sugar cane to the dark greens of the forested hills, is a far cry from the 'desert island paradise' of the imagination.

These are the other Cubas – beaches of white sand lapped by the warm waters of the Atlantic and Caribbean; ranges of hills, their flanks draped with lush vegetation; swamplands where crocodiles and rare birds are still found; old towns with glorious colonial centres; and fields of sugar cane, tobacco, coffee and lush grass where *guajiros* (farmers) tend the crops and *vaqueros* (cowboys) herd the cattle. Cuba is many lands, each one a fascinating place that will leave a lasting impression on the heart and mind of the visitor.

Cienfuegos' main square has some of Cuba's best-preserved colonial buildings

Cuba's Features

Geography
• Cuba is the largest of the Caribbean islands, and the world's 15th largest island. It is 1,250km long and 32–190km wide. There are 5,760km of coast, much of it white sand beaches, and over 4,000 offshore islands.

Climate
• Cuba has only two seasons, the rainy season from May to October, and the dry season from November to April. The rainy season is the hottest, with an average daytime temperature of about 30°C; humidity is usually around 70 per cent. In the dry season the average daytime temperature is 25°C, with a humidity of about 60 per cent. October and November is the hurricane season.

Population
• Cuba has 11 million inhabitants, about 2 million of whom live in Havana. There are an estimated 1½ million Cuban exiles living in the US, most of them in Florida.

Economy
• Tourism is Cuba's largest source of foreign currency, along with sugar, nickel and fishing. 'Modern' industries include biotechnology and pharmaceuticals.

In 1959 over 70 per cent of Cuba's trade was with the US. After the revolution this fell to less than 5 per cent, over 80 per cent then being with the USSR. Since the collapse of the Soviet Union, Canada, Mexico, Japan and the European Union have become Cuba's most important trading partners.

People
Cuba's native population of Amerindians was wiped out by the Spanish settlers. Today's Cubans are a mix of colonial Spanish and African slaves. Officially the country is 66 per cent white, 22 per cent mixed race and 12 per cent black, but as visitors will soon realise, the terms are easier to define than the differences are to spot.

Tourism
At present almost 2 million tourists visit Cuba each year compared to the 10 million who visit the nearby Bahamas. Interestingly, the tourist:local ratio is one tourist for every 15 locals in Cuba, but 15 tourists for every one local in the Bahamas.

The finest tobacco comes from the Viñales region

Essence of Cuba

Below: *a typical Moorish detail from Manzanillo*
Bottom: *the vast Parque Baconao, to the east of Santiago de Cuba, offers splendid beaches as well as greenery*

Countries tend to be defined by their climates and histories, but in Cuba those two elements have produced a country that transcends the cliché. Almost nothing remains of Cuba's Amerindians, but all subsequent settlers have left their mark. The Spanish built magnificent palaces and churches, the British laid out central Havana on a grand scale, and African slaves brought a culture that is still the vital pulse of modern Cuba. The barriers to travel, raised after the revolution, are now coming down, allowing visitors to experience not only the fine historical blend that makes up Cuba's people and architecture, but the joys of its climate – long, sunny days for enjoying beautiful beaches and warm seas, or exploring some of the Caribbean's most spectacular scenery.

THE **10** ESSENTIALS

If you only have a short time to visit Cuba, and would like to sample the very best that the country has to offer, here are the essentials:

• **Visit a Casa de la Trova.** Every town and sizeable village has such a house. Here local bands will play while other locals sing or dance.

• **Visit a revolutionary site.** Visitors arriving at Havana's José Martí Airport are greeted by the slogan *Creemos en la Revolución* – We believe in the revolution. To understand Cuba the visitor must understand the revolution.

• **Buy a T-shirt.** Cuban T-shirts, especially those decorated with revolutionary slogans or pictures of Che Guevara, are among the most attractive to be found anywhere and are the essential souvenir.

• **Visit a site on the Hemingway Trail.** Most of the best work by one the century's most influential writers was written in Cuba. His house is the target for true pilgrims, but even casual readers can pay homage at La Bodeguita del Medio.

• **Visit a cigar factory.** Despite the trade difficulties, Havana cigars are still the world standard. Even non-smokers will find a visit fascinating.

• **To gain an insight into the real Cuba,** try visiting the market in Matanzas if you are staying in Varadero, or visit Baracoa if you are in Santiago or Guardalavaca.

• **Go for a swim.** You haven't experienced Cuba until you have submerged yourself in the warm, turquoise waters of the Atlantic or Caribbean.

• **Sample a Cuban ice-cream.** Food is rationed in Cuba, making some restaurants disappointing, but the island still has wonderful ice-cream. Try the coconut (the best) or mango flavours.

• **Take a stroll through Old Havana.** No trip would be complete without a visit to this magical quarter.

• **Take a rum cocktail** to the beach on your last night and watch the sun go down towards Mexico.

Cubans are very proud of their musical heritage and visitors will often be entertained by impromptu concerts

No one should miss the chance of trying some local ice-cream

9

The Shaping of Cuba

c3500 BC
Siboney and Guanahataby Amerindians from the northern coast of South America are Cuba's first human visitors.

AD 1200
Taino Arawak Amerindians arrive in Cuba from Hispaniola (now Haiti and the Dominican Republic).

1492
Christopher Columbus lands on Cuba's northern coast believing he has reached Japan.

1511
Diego Velázquez founds the first Spanish settlement on Cuba, at Baracoa.

1515
The first seven *villas* (garrison towns) are established on the island. In 1515 Santiago de Cuba replaces Baracoa as the island's capital. The Spaniards annihilate the Amerindian population, despite brave resistance.

1518
Hernando Córtez leaves Santiago de Cuba for the conquest of the Aztec Empire of Mexico.

De Céspedes is one of Cuba's most revered heroes

10

1519
Havana established, although Santiago remains as the island's capital.

1522
The first slaves are brought to the island from Africa.

1555
Havana is sacked by French pirates. Despite this, the island's captain general moves to the city in 1556, strengthening its defences.

1607
Havana is formally declared capital.

1762
The British capture Havana and take control of Cuba. British occupation lasts for only 11 months, at the end of which the island is exchanged for Florida and returns to Spanish rule.

1790–1810
Massive influx of African slaves and expansion of the sugar industry mean that sugar becomes Cuba's major export.

1850
The Cuban flag is raised for the first time at Cárdenas during a failed coup.

1865
The importation of African slaves ceases.

1868–78
The first War of Independence is launched by Carlos Manuel de Céspedes, near Manzanillo. Despite the rebels' defeat, Spanish rule is weakened and slavery is abolished in 1886.

1895–98
The second War of Independence is launched following a

1961
A US-backed invasion by anti-Castro Cuban exiles fails at the Bay of Pigs.

1962
Cuban Missile Crisis. With Castro's agreement Soviet leader Nikita Khrushchev decides to place Soviet missiles on the island. President Kennedy orders the US navy to stop Soviet missile-carrying ships and for a few days in October the world hovers on the edge of nuclear war.

1980
About 125,000 Cubans leave for the US in the 'Mariel' boat-lift.

1990
Tourism exceeds sugar as the island's major dollar earner but economic difficulties force Castro to declare the 'Special Period' of austerity.

1999
Five-year-old Elian Gonzalez becomes a *cause célèbre* when he is found afloat in the sea after the boat carrying him to Florida sinks, drowning his mother. An emotional custody battle ensues between his Florida relatives and his Cuban father. His father wins the day, and Elian flies home in June 2000.

long propaganda war by José Martí. In 1898 the US battleship *Maine* blows up in Havana harbour precipitating the Spanish-American War. US troops land near Santiago de Cuba and the Spanish surrender.

1902
After four years of US military occupation Cuba becomes independent.

1903
As part of the independence declaration, Cuba is required to allow the US to set up the Guantánamo Naval Base.

1952
After a series of tyrannical dictators, Fulgencio Batista, a former army chief-of-staff, takes power in a military coup.

1953
Fidel Castro launches an attack on the Moncada

Havana's baroque cathedral and the square in which it stands have changed little in 250 years

Barracks in Santiago de Cuba. Castro is captured and imprisoned for two years, then exiled to Mexico.

1956
Fidel Castro, Che Guevara and 80 other rebels land near Cabo Cruz from the motorboat *Granma*. Most are killed, but Castro and Guevara survive and take refuge in the Sierra Maestra.

1958
Che Guevara takes Santa Clara in the decisive battle of the revolution.

1959
On 1 January Batista flees Cuba and Fidel Castro assumes power. The US places an economic embargo on Cuba.

11

Peace & Quiet

The hibiscus is just one species that flourishes in this botanists' paradise

Cuba is the most unspoilt island in the Caribbean, having undergone virtually no development. In many towns and almost all villages, the horse and cart is still the primary means of transport. Outside Havana, Varadero, Santiago and a handful of tourist sites, it could be said that all of Cuba is a haven of peace and quiet, where the pace of life is relaxed – provided your idyll is not disturbed by locals pestering you for chewing gum or soap.

Wilderness Walking

For true peace, go to some of Cuba's many wild areas. But before heading off into the wilderness please be cautious: there are no official trails, few and often poor maps, and limited transport, accommodation, food and drink – even rescue services. Take all you will need, make transport arrangements beforehand and come back the way you went out. The best places for walking are the Sierra Maestra near Santiago, the Escambray Mountains between Trinidad and Cienfuegos, the Viñales Valley near Pinar del Río and almost any section of undeveloped coastline. The Zapata peninsula is Cuba's most important wildlife area, but access to it is difficult and visitors will need a guide, or to join a guided tour.

Plant Life

There are 6,700 plant species on the island, about half of them found nowhere else on earth. The national tree is the *palm real* (royal palm), which can reach a height of 30m. Though there are still some hardwood trees, the visitor is much more likely to see palms, flame trees (with their distinctive scimitar-like seed pods) and bougainvillaea. The national flower is the *mariposa* (butterfly jasmine), and the hundreds of other flower species inlude myriad orchids, many of them endemic.

Animal Life

Cuba's 350-odd species of bird range from the bee hummingbird (known as the *zunzuncito*), the world's smallest bird, to flamingos and pelicans. The national bird is the parrot-like trogon, adopted because of its largely red, white and blue plumage, which mirrors the national flag. Birds that visitors are most likely to see are the grackle, a striking black bird with a curious

V-shaped tail, the beige and white mockingbird, which favours hotel gardens, and the turkey vulture.

There are turtles in the seas off Cuba, terrapins in the lakes, axolotls, salamanders and many types of frog, some unknown elsewhere. The largest reptile is the Cuban boa (*majá*) which can reach 4m, but the one most commonly seen by visitors is the iguana (Cayo Largo is the place to see them). On the mainland, particularly on the northern coast, visitors may also see the curious curl-tailed lizard (confusingly called an iguana by the locals). Cuba has its own species of crocodile (*Crocodylus rhombifer*), claimed to be the world's most aggressive. It can leap up to 2m into the air to pluck *jutías* from trees.

The *jutía* is a large tree rat, up to 65cm long and weighing around 4kg. It is hunted by Cubans, and is now only found on certains cays and in mangrove swamps. Even rarer is the *almiqui* or Cuban solenodon, a tiny insect-eating mammal thought to be extinct until it was 'rediscovered' in 1974.

Of other rarities, the Cuba Greta is one of only two species of butterfly with transparent wings, while the colourful polymita snail is found only on Cuba.

Below: few visitors will leave the island without having seen (or heard) a grackle
Bottom: the Sierra Maestra is typical of Cuba's undeveloped countryside

Cuba's Famous

A popular name for Castro is El Barbudo (the Bearded One); Cubans sometimes stroke their chin to refer to him silently

Fidel Castro

The third of seven children of a sugar farmer, Fidel Castro Ruz was born in 1927 in Finca Las Manacas, a farmhouse near the village of Biran, which lies southeast of Holguín. He attended Catholic and Jesuit schools, then went to Havana University in 1945 to study law. He became the centre of a group of dissidents who came together with the intention of overthrowing the dictator Batista, and burst on to the Cuban stage on 26 July 1953 as the leader of the attack on the Moncada Barracks. After capture and imprisonment, he was exiled to Mexico, where he met Che Guevara. In 1956 they and 80 others – including Fidel's younger brother (and now heir apparent) Raúl – boarded the *Granma* to return to Cuba. This and other aspects of the revolution that followed are explored, where relevant, throughout the book.

Olympic Champions
Teofilo Stevenson won the heavyweight boxing title at the 1972, 1976 and 1980 Olympics, and was also world amateur champion, a truly remarkable record. Stevenson was the first of many great Cuban champions – Alberto Juantorena won the 400m/800m Olympic double in 1976, the first man ever to do so, and Javier Sotomayor is the world record holder in the high jump, though his Olympic career has been marred by drug allegations.

Che Guevara

Ernesto ('Che') Guevara was an Argentinian, born in 1928 of middle-class parents and destined to be a doctor until his awakening to the horrors of poverty in Latin America led him down the revolutionary trail. After spending time in Guatemala he moved to Mexico, where he met Fidel Castro. After the success of the revolution, Che took Cuban citizenship and a place in Castro's government, but his desire for direct action eventually led him to Bolivia to incite revolution. There, in October 1967, he was captured and summarily executed. Che might have been just another fighter in the revolution but for the chance shot (a single 35mm frame) taken by Alberto Korda at a rally in Havana. The young, handsome, bearded face in a black beret became a 1960s icon. No student's wall was without the image and the face still looks out from many Cuban souvenirs.

Marxist idealist and fearless fighter, Che was dedicated to the overthrow of imperialism

14

Top Ten

Above: *Crocodile farm, Zapata peninsula*

15

1
Catedral de la Habana

Havana's cathedral is now the symbol of Cuba's religious revival

Dominating an airy square at the heart of old Havana is one of the island's most distinctive buildings.

✠ 33C4

✉ Plaza de la Catedral

🕐 Mon–Fri 9–11, 2–6 and Sun mornings for Mass, but these times are notoriously erratic

🍴 El Patio (£££), Plaza de la Catedral

🚌 Plaza de la Catedral is on several of Havana's bus routes

ℹ Infatur, Obispo 252 esq Cuba ☎ 861 1544

♿ None

🎫 Free

↔ Museo de Arte Colonial (► 44)

Though it is known 'officially' as the Catedral de la Habana, many Cubans refer to it as San Cristóbal. On 15 January 1796 a boat dropped anchor in Havana's harbour and a velvet-draped coffin was rowed ashore. The coffin, believed to hold the remains of Christopher Columbus (Cristóbal Colón), was transferred to the cathedral. The small lead casket inside contained only a small quantity of dust and a bone fragment, but was laid below a marble slab and became a focus for ceremony. It is now accepted that the remains, which were shipped back to Spain in 1899, were probably those of Columbus' son, Diego.

The cathedral was begun by the Jesuits in 1748, their first task being the draining of an area of swamp. In 1767, with the building still unfinished, the Jesuits were expelled from all Spanish territory by King Carlos III. After a five-year gap, work began again and was completed in 1777. The façade is the finest example of baroque architecture in Cuba and has been described as the most beautiful in Latin America, and as 'music turned to stone'. Others find the façade over-elaborate to the point of vulgarity. One curiosity is the two quite dissimilar bell-towers, strangely at odds with the absolutely symmetrical façade.

The cathedral's interior is austere, having been stripped of much of its finery. Only the altar, with its Carrara marble, onyx and gold and silver inlay, suggests the treasure that could once be found here.

2
Cojímar

Politics aside, the most famous inhabitant of Cuba was not a Cuban, but the American writer Ernest Hemingway.

Ernest Miller Hemingway was born in 1899 and worked as a journalist before becoming a full-time writer. He was in Spain during the Civil War, then moved to Cuba. He stayed on the island for over 20 years, only moving when ill health and the deterioration of relations between the US and Cuba made it impossible for him to stay. Shortly after his departure to the US in 1961 he committed suicide.

There is an unofficial Hemingway Trail in Cuba, with literary pilgrims visiting his house – now a museum (► 49) – and his favourite bars, and attempting to locate the places mentioned in *Islands in the Stream*. But best of all is the fishing village of Cojímar. Here Hemingway moored *Pilar*, a 12m boat named for the patron saint of Zaragoza, which he used to fish for blue marlin, the largest and bravest of the Caribbean's great game fish. At Cojímar Hemingway met Gregorio Fuentes, who captained the *Pilar* until the writer left Cuba. The last time the pair used the boat was in a marlin competition in May 1960 – won by Fidel Castro. It is usually said that Fuentes was the inspiration for Santiago, the hero of *The Old Man and the Sea*, which won Hemingway the Nobel Prize in 1954.

A bust of the author looks out from the columned memorial beside the La Chorrera fort. Gregorio Fuentes was named a national hero by Fidel Castro in 1993, he regaled visitors with tales of Hemingway until he died in 2002.

To the east of Cojímar – follow the main coast road past the port – are the Playas del Este, a series of half a dozen beaches backed by resort hotels. Though mostly catering for package tourists, the beaches are within easy reach of Havana and are well worth a day trip.

28B3

About 10km east of Havana

La Terraza (££), Hemingway's favourite restaurant. Restored by Castro as a memorial to the author, it is one of Cuba's best seafood restaurants

Regular service (No 58) from Havana

Few

The bust of Hemingway at La Chorrera was made from melted-down bronze propellers donated by local fishermen

17

3
El Cobre

The statue of Cuba's patron saint, the Virgin of Charity, is found in this remote, but exquisite, church.

29E1

El Cobre stands above the village of Cobre, 19km northwest of Santiago de Cuba

362446

The Hospedaría (£), built to accommodate pilgrims, serves excellent meals

Services from the bus station at Santiago de Cuba

Plaza de Martí, Santiago de Cuba 623302

None

Free, but an offering to the church is welcomed

In 1608 three boys were fishing in Nipe Bay, off the north Cuban coast, when a sudden storm threatened their boat. They noticed something floating by and hauled it in to discover a statue of a mulatto Virgin bearing the inscription 'I am the Virgin of Charity'. The storm abruptly ended and the boys were safe. Legend has it that the statue – in wood and about 30cm high – was given to a Cuban Indian chief by a Spanish conquistador in about 1510.

The lovely church in Cobre that now houses the statue is Cuba's only basilica and is in a beautiful setting, its cream walls and towers contrasting with the green hills beyond. It dates largely from a major rebuilding in the 1920s. The Virgin of Charity was declared the patron saint of Cuba in 1916, and the new church was consecrated on the saint's day, 8 September, in 1927.

Beside the church are the Stations of the Cross. Inside, stairs lead to a glass case in which stands the statue, clothed in a cloak of satin embellished with gold. There is a remarkable and varied collection of votive offerings from pilgrims. The site is also important to followers of Santería (► 35), for whom the statue represents the goddess Ochún.

The negative aspect to El Cobre is the youths trying to sell souvenirs and pyrites. Some years ago the authorities closed the site to tourists after one visitor was attacked and robbed. Things are better now, but do be careful.

El Cobre once housed Hemingway's Nobel medallion, but this has now been removed for safe keeping

4
Escambray Mountains

Though not the highest mountain range in Cuba, the Escambray is the most beautiful, its purple peaks rising above lush green foothills.

Cuba is not a mountainous country: its highest peak, Pico Turquino in the Sierra Maestra to the west of Santiago de Cuba, rises to just 1,972m, many metres lower than Blue Mountain on the much smaller neighbouring island of Jamaica. Escambray is the second highest range, its highest peak, Pico de San Juan, rising to only 1,156m. The peaks are covered in lush rainforest that is home to a remarkable number of plant and animal species.

The Escambray can be explored on foot, though the lack of maps and trails makes this inadvisable. Despite the attractions of the rainforest and some of the finest water-falls in the Americas, it is better to confine an exploration to the roads. Though few, these do pass through some of the most spectacular scenery; it is arguable whether the best view of the Escambray is to be had from the *autopista* linking Santa Clara and Ciego de Avila, or from the coast road that links Trinidad and Cienfuegos.

From Santa Clara (▶ 80–81), go south to Manicaragua, then south again to the vast reservoir of Lake Hanabanilla. Here boats can be hired and well-marked trails can be followed into the forest. An alternative trip is to Topes de Collantes, a mountain resort built originally as a sanatorium for tuberculosis sufferers. Topes lies about 20km northwest of Trinidad. From the resort a road heads west to La Sierrita, passing close to the high point of Pico de San Juan. From this road the view towards the Caribbean is magnificent.

28C2

Between Santa Clara and Trinidad

🍴 El Río Negro (££) on Lake Hanabanilla – reached by boat or a walk from the Hotel Hanabanilla – or the Hotel Los Pinos at Topes de Collantes (££)

🚌 Infrequent buses reach Lake Hanabanilla (from Manicaragua) and Topes (from Trinidad)

❓ Boat excursions are possible on Lake Hanabanilla from the Hotel Hanabanilla

To the north the Escambray Mountains tower over Lake Hanabanilla

5
The Malecón, Havana

32A5

La Casona Del 17 (£)
Calle 17, 60 e/ N y M

On several of Havana's
bus routes

Calle 23 (La Rampa)
esq Γ ☎ 070 7031/
870 5284

Good

On calm days, on stormy days, by moonlight or in the sun, Havana's Malecón offers a superb walk.

Malecón means jetty, the original purpose of the massive construction that runs for almost 5km from the mouth of the Río Almendares to the Castillo de la Punta having been to keep the Atlantic Ocean out of the new city of Havana. There has been a sea wall here for centuries, the present structure is to the design of a Cuban engineer named Albear, whose 1857 plan was not completed until 1902. Correctly the road that runs beside the wall is the Avenida Antonio Máceo, but if you ask for that rather than the Malecón it is likely that the response will be a blank stare.

The Malecón carries a six-lane road, but the traffic that once thundered along it is now largely a memory, leaving promenaders to enjoy the hiss of the waves as they retreat from the wall. On calm days the sun sparkles off the sea; lovers stroll arm in arm; fishermen cast their lines from the wall edge; and there may even be a few hardy

Above: *on sunny days the Malecón is a popular meeting place and 'beach' for young Cubans*

Right: *the castle of San Salvador de la Punta guards the entrance to Havana's harbour*

Habaneros hurling themselves off the wall in car tyre inner tubes. Rumour has it that some of those will be trying to get to Florida, but that seems unlikely. More likely is that they believe being closer to the fish will improve their luck.

On stormy days the Atlantic thunders its way across the rocks below the wall, smashing into the masonry and sending spectacular plumes of spray across the road. The façades of the buildings lining the Malecón were a decaying testament to the power and corrosive nature of the sea, but they are now being extensively restored with help from Spain, Portugal and UNESCO .

If you have limited time, come around sunset and follow the promenade in Vedado, from the memorial to Antonio Máceo (a hero of the Second War of Independence) to the monument for the USS *Maine,* whose sinking sparked the Spanish-American War. On the inland side of the fine arc that is this section of the Malecón is an array of buildings dating from the early years of the twentieth century. On the seaward side you will encounter groups of young Cubans chatting and laughing, while courting couples listen to the sea.

Some buildings still resist the combined onslaught of salt spray and neglect

6
Museo de la Revolución, Havana

Housed in one of Havana's most sumptuous buildings, this museum is the best place to start exploring the history of the revolution.

✝ 32B4

✉ Refugio 1 e/ Monserrate y Zulueta

☎ 862 4091

🕐 Tue 10–6, Wed–Sun 10–5

🍴 None in museum. La Piña de Plata (£), corner of Calle Monserrate and Calle Obispo; or Café on ground floor of Hotel Sevilla on Prado y Trocadero

🚌 On several of Havana's bus routes

ℹ Montana de Gómez, by Parque Central ☎ 863 6960

♿ Few   🖐 Moderate

In 1913, close to a section of the old city walls, work began on the building of a parliament house for the provincial government. By the time the work was completed in 1920 the building had been taken over by the President. It remained the Palacio Presidencial until 1959, when Fulgencio Batista fled from it as Castro's forces secured the country.

The building has been described as looking like a wedding cake, and you either love its ostentatious grandeur or loathe its vulgarity. Tiffany's of New York created an extravagant interior that matched the ornate exterior, though much of their work has been stripped out.

It is impossible to view everything in one visit, but there are items that should not be missed: Che Guevara's black beret; an extraordinary diorama of Che and Camilo Cienfuegos in the Sierra Maestra, the full-size wax models complete with their actual horses, stuffed after death; and a collection of clothing, suitably blood-stained and including Fidel Castro's trousers. The history of Cuba from its first islanders through Spanish rule to independence is well presented, though the collection of post-revolution statistics is rather hard going. Light relief is offered by *El Rincon de los Cretinos* (the Corner of Cretins) with cartoons ridiculing Batista and US presidents Reagan and Bush. On the square at the front of the museum is the tank used by Fidel Castro at the Bay of Pigs. Visible from outside is Castro's invasion boat, the *Granma* (► 40), but it can only be viewed at close quarters from inside the museum.

This grand building was once the presidential palace

7

Parque Céspedes, Santiago de Cuba

This beautiful and historic park at the heart of Cuba's second city was named in honour of Carlos Manuel de Céspedes.

The park's shaded centre is a welcome retreat on the hottest days

In October 1868, Céspedes freed the slaves on the sugar plantation he owned near Manzanillo, sparking the First War of Liberation against Spanish rule. Some experts say that a third of a million people died in this bloody, ten-year war and Cuba's sugar industry was virtually destroyed. The war marked the beginning of the end of colonial power: within eight years slavery had been abolished, and within another dozen the Spanish had gone. Céspedes, murdered (while playing chess) at the end of the war, was buried in Santiago. It was in the Parque that Fidel Castro gave his first speech as Cuba's leader on 1 January 1959.

There is a memorial to Céspedes in the square, but to reach it you will need to negotiate a crowd: Parque Céspedes is small and delightfully tree-shaded, and understandably popular with the people of Santiago. On a good day there will be impromptu concerts from local musicians, children enjoying rides in goat-carts, animated conversations and people just watching the world go by.

On the Parque's western side is **Casa de Velázquez**, reputedly built by Diego Velázquez, who founded the city in 1515. Much restored, the building is claimed to be the oldest in the whole of Latin America. The first floor has a balcony with a wooden grille, a distinctly Moorish feature. On this floor Velázquez had his offices. Later the house was occupied by Hernando Córtez. Casa Velázquez is now a museum, with some original furnishings and other items from Cuba's colonial past. The other sides of the square are occupied by equally fascinating buildings.

86B1

Santiago is linked by long-distance bus to Havana and other major cities

Santiago is on the main cross-island railway line

Santiago is linked by air to Havana and other major cities

Parque Céspedes, by the cathedral

None

Casa de Velázquez (Museo de Ambiente Histórico Cubano)

Parque Céspedes

(0226) 652 652

Mon–Sat 9–5, Sun 9–1

Café La Isabelica (£) in Plaza de Dolores

Moderate

23

8
Trinidad

With its narrow, cobbled streets, red-tiled
houses and delightful main square, Trinidad is
the pearl of Cuba.

On Christmas Day 1514, on the orders of Diego Velázquez, a Mass was held under a tree on the site of Cuba's third *villa* (garrison town, ➤ 10), and Velázquez named the site after the Holy Trinity (Santísima Trinidad). The town's position, shielded from the gaze of the rest of Cuba by the Escambray Mountains, meant that smuggling was a profitable activity, adding to the wealth of the local sugar mills and resulting in an array of beautiful buildings. In 1988 UNESCO proclaimed Trinidad a World Heritage Site.

Unusually for Cuban towns, Trinidad was not laid out on a grid, the builders preferring to organise the streets so that one side was always in the shade. At the heart of the old town is Plaza Mayor, with Parque Marte at its centre. The open park is the sunniest spot in town, the tall, elegant palms offering little shade. The roads around the square – and elsewhere in town – are cobbled (which dissuades cyclists) and closed to traffic, so the visitor is free to enjoy the sights untroubled by anything except local hustlers.

On the northeastern side of the square is the late 19th-century Church of the Holy Trinity, in Romanesque style. Also facing the square is a collection of exquisite colonial buildings, some of which house excellent museums. The Museo Arquitectura Colonial explores Trinidad's history; the Museo Romántico has a magnificent collection of late 18th- and early 19th-century furnishings and furniture; and finally the Museo de Arqueología Guamuhaya explores Cuba's Indian past and natural history.

The Parque Marte at the heart of Trinidad is framed by elegant Spanish-style villas

9
Varadero Peninsula

Varadero is the tourist capital of Cuba with all that entails, but the negative aspects of its development cannot hide its beauty.

On the north coast of Cuba, about 145km east of Havana, a narrow peninsula of sand points like a crooked finger into the Atlantic Ocean. This is Varadero, the tourist centre of Cuba. Around the turn of the century, rich Habaneros had second homes on the northern shore, while fishermen worked the beaches of the south. Then, in 1926, Irénée Du Pont of the French-American chemical giant bought the peninsula, built himself a home and persuaded other rich Americans to join him. Du Pont's house – Xanadu – is now the Las Américas restaurant, and it is the diners who enjoy the marvellous sea views.

After the revolution Varadero's fortunes fell, but they have been revived by the need for foreign tourist currency. The peninsula's growing array of hotels, restaurants and bars, are the products of this need. Toll checkpoints on the only road in and out make the resort effectively off-limits to Cubans. The nodding donkeys and gas flare of the Varadero oil field are yet another aspect of the island's economy. But there is still much to enjoy. It is no tourist literature hyperbole to say that palm trees fringe beaches of white sand, which are lapped by the warm, turquoise waters of a sea with an average annual temperature of 25°C.

Elsewhere on the peninsula, the Cueva de Ambrosio is decorated with the most important pictographs and drawings so far discovered from Cuba's Indian past. Parque Josone is a peaceful landscaped park with a lake and cafés, while in Varadero Natural Park, at the very tip of the peninsula, the natural landscape (including some as yet untouched beach) has been preserved.

28C3

Off Cuba's north coast, about 145km east of Havana

Many possibilities. Las Américas (££), at Avenida Las Américas is worth a visit for its décor and history

Regular buses to Varadero from Havana and Matanzas

Regular flights to Havana from the airport to the southwest of the peninsula

Corner of Avenida Primera (sometimes written Avenida 1er) and Calle 23

Few

Looking past an Amerindian-style sculpture to the Du Pont mansion

10
Zapata Peninsula

✚ 28B2

✉ To the west of the Bay of Pigs

⏱ Tours of the reserves near the Bay of Pigs are available daily from Playa Larga and Playa Girón

🍴 There are good restaurants at Guamá and Bohío de Don Pedro signposted at km 142 of the Carreteria Central

🚌 Several buses daily from Jagüey Grande reach Playa Larga. Daily buses link Playa Larga and Playa Girón

♿ None

✋ Moderate

As with many other islands, Cuba is rich in endemic plants and animals, and Zapata is the showcase site for these.

The Spaniards named the swampy peninsula to the west of the Bay of Pigs after its likeness to a shoe (*zapato*). Underlying it is a sheet of limestone, barely above sea-level: the swamp is flooded during the wet season, and in long dry periods a layer of peat is exposed which moves in a sinister fashion when walked on. Hardwood forests once flourished; charcoal burning has thinned these and some logging is still allowed, but at the western tip of Zapata a National Park has been set up to protect the wilderness.

Around 90 per cent of Cuba's bird species can be found on the peninsula, including flamingos and the bee hummingbird, the world's smallest bird. The rare Zapata wren and Zapata rail occur nowhere else on earth. The wren, an inconspicuous greyish-brown bird, has a fine song. The rail is sometimes heard by lucky visitors, but the bird is rarely seen – even by those studying it.

Zapata is home to the Cuban crocodile, once on the verge of extinction (in part because of hybridisation with the more common American crocodile) but now bred on special reserves. The peninsula is one of the last strongholds of the West Indian manatee, the rarest type of this large, slow-moving aquatic mammal.

Sightseeing trips into the swamp are possible when accompanied by official guides – information and permits are available from the National Park Office in Playa Larga (☎ 459 7249). Avid birdwatchers should go to the Santo Tomás reserve west of Playa Larga at the head of the Bay of Pigs, or the Las Salinas reserve on the western side of the bay.

The Zapata swamps are home to some of the world's rarest birds and animals, but are best visited by boat

What
to See

Above: *Havana's
modern skyline from
La Cabaña*

27

CUBA

Havana-Vedado (seen here
from the Capri Hotel) was
built by American
gangsters and reminds
many visitors of Miami

Havana & Environs

Starting as a collection of wooden huts beside a natural harbour, Havana rapidly grew to be the jewel in Europe's New World crown. The Havana of the *conquistadores* was an opulent city that reflected the glories of Spain and the confidence in Spanish mastery of Latin America.

The wealth of the sugar trade, built on the backs of African slaves, maintained Havana's fortunes. With the end of colonial rule it became a glitzy but slightly seedy place, controlled by US gangsters and a playground for their rich, but tasteless, clients. In the years of economic struggle that followed the events of 1958 the city lost its shine, but took on an almost mystical air, its inaccessibility making it seem as the fabled cities of the Orient did to medieval Europeans.

Now Havana is open again, and the myth is justified. Despite the decay, Old Havana is as gracious as was claimed, and the newer city as elegant as any in Latin America.

' One of the provinces is called Avan, and there the people are born with tails. '

CHRISTOPHER COLUMBUS
in a letter dated
15 February 1493

Old & Central Havana

Habana Vieja – Old Havana – was built by the Spanish in the 16th and 17th centuries; many buildings survive from that period, though Cuba's recent economic problems have meant that some have been lost, neglect leading to their collapse or demolition. In 1982 UNESCO declared Old Havana a World Heritage Site and began a programme of stabilising and restoring the old palaces, houses and churches. It will be worth while: Old Havana is not only a city of great beauty, but one of great character, which should be explored at a leisurely pace, taking time to discover its delightful hidden corners.

Central Havana, on the other hand, was built in the 18th century to a design of the British, and is a more open part of the city, the extra space available beyond the city walls allowing more, and bigger, public spaces.

What to See in Old & Central Havana

CALLE OBISPO ✪✪✪

This is Old Havana's main street, linking the Plaza de Armas with Parque Central. It is traffic free (if you discount the cyclists) and lined with shops and stalls, adding souvenir hunting to the delights of the architecture (though some of the modern additions, most especially the Ministry of Education, are hardly in keeping with the subtleties of the older buildings). Heading west from Plaza de Armas, the first gem is No 117–119, built in the mid-17th century and claimed to be the oldest house in the city. With its plant-hung balcony it is a delight. Inside (it is occupied by a bookshop) look out for the ceilings, which show a distinct Moorish influence. No 113 houses a small museum of silverware, while at the corner of Obispo and Mercadares the **Sala de la Revolución** (reached up a private-looking stairway) sets the Cuban revolution in the context of other popular uprisings. Next on the left is the Hotel Ambos Mundos (➤ 38). Further on towards Parque Central the neo-classical building erected for the Bank of New York is now occupied by the State Finance Committee. A museum in its basement has a collection of Cuban banknotes from colonial times to the present. Diagonally opposite the bank building, Casa Gómez, built in 1836 for a rich merchant, now houses a tourist information office.

✚ 32B3
🍴 Cafe Paris (£), Calle Obispo 202

Sala de la Revolucion
✚ 33C3
✉ Calle Obispo 151
🕐 Tue–Sat 10:30–6, Sun 9–1
♿ None
🎟 Free

Above: *the Gran Teatro seen from the Hotel Inglaterra*

There is a flea market Tuesday to Sunday at Tacon, a block south of Plaza de la Catedral

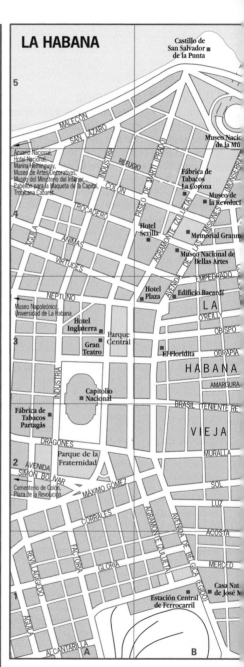

LA HABANA

Castillo de San Salvador de la Punta

MALECÓN

SAN LÁZARO

REFUGIO

Museo Nacional de la Mú

Acuario Nacional,
Hotel Nacional,
Marina Hemingway,
Museo de Artes Decorativas,
Museo del Ministerio del Interior,
Pabellón para la Maqueta de la Capital,
Tropicana Cabaret

COLÓN

INDUSTRIA

PASEO DE MARTÍ (PRADO)

AGRAMONTE (ZULUETA)

MISIONES

MONSERRATE

Fábrica de Tabacos La Corona

Museo de la Revolución

TROCADERO

Hotel Sevilla

Memorial Granma

ANIMAS

AGUILA

VIRTUDES

Museo Nacional de Bellas Artes

NEPTUNO

Museo Napoleónico,
Universidad de La Habana

Hotel Plaza

AVENIDA

EMPEDRADO

Edificio Bacardí

LA

O'REILLY

Hotel Inglaterra

Parque Central

OBISPO

Gran Teatro

El Floridita

OBRAPIA

INDUSTRIA

HABANA

AMARGURA

Capitolio Nacional

BRASIL (TENIENTE REY)

Fábrica de Tabacos Partagás

VIEJA

DRAGONES

Parque de la Fraternidad

MURALLA

AVENIDA SIMÓN BOLÍVAR

Cementerio de Colón,
Plaza de la Revolución

MÁXIMO GÓMEZ

SOL

LUZ

CORRALES

AGRAMONTE (ZULUETA)

AVENIDA DE BÉLGICA (EGIDO)

ACOSTA

FACTORÍA

REVILLAGIGEDO

GLORIA

MERCED

AGUILA

Casa Natal de José Martí

Estación Central de Ferrocarril

ALCANTARILLA

A

B

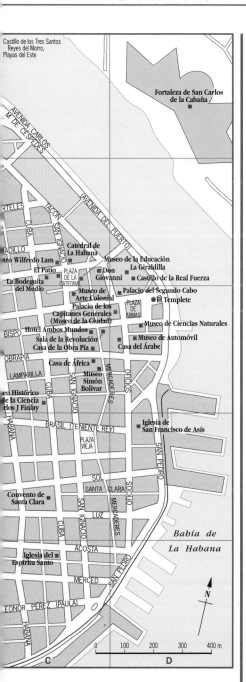

Castillo de los Tres Santos
Reyes del Morro,
Playas del Este

Fortaleza de San Carlos
de la Cabaña

AVENIDA CARLOS
M DE CESPEDES

AVENIDA DEL PUERTO

RTELES

TACON

CUBA

SAN IGNACIO

ADILLO
tro Wilfredo Lam

Catedral de
La Habana

Museo de la Educación

El Patio   La Giraldilla

PLAZA   Don
DE LA   Giovanni   Castillo de la Real Fuerza
CATEDRAL

La Bodeguita
del Medio

Museo de
Arte Colonial   Palacio del Segundo Cabo

Palacio de los   El Templete
Capitanes Generales   PLAZA
(Museo de la Ciudad)   DE
BISPO   ARMAS

Hotel Ambos Mundos   Museo de Ciencias Naturales

Sala de la Revolución   Museo de Automóvil

OBRAPIA   Casa de la Obra Pía   Casa del Árabe

Casa de África

LAMPARILLA   Museo
Simón
Bolívar

CUBA   SAN IGNACIO   MERCADERES   OFICIOS

co Histórico
e la Ciencia
rlos J Finlay

HABANA   BRASIL (TENIENTE REY)

PLAZA   Iglesia de
VIEJA   San Francisco de Asís

SAN PEDRO

SOL

SANTA CLARA   SOCIICHO

Convento de   SAN IGNACIO   MERCADERES
Santa Clara   LUZ

CUBA

ACOSTA   Bahía de
La Habana

Iglesia del
Espíritu Santo

MERCED

SAN PEDRO

EONOR PEREZ (PAULA)

HABANA

N

0   100   200   300   400 m

C   D

*Groups of statues
represent the performing
arts on the façade of the
Gran Teatro*

33

> ## *Did you know ?*
> *Santería, the 'Rule of Saints', is followed by*
> *as many as 5 million Cubans. Of African origin, the*
> *religion has hundreds of orishas (gods and goddesses),*
> *many of them identified with Christian saints.*
> *Santería places a strict code of conduct on its*
> *followers, who can often be recognised by their*
> *necklaces and bracelets of coloured beads.*

CAPITOLIO NACIONAL ✪

32A3
South of Parque Central
860 3411
Guided tours Mon–Sat 9–5
Buses 232 and 264
Few
Moderate

Visitors who have also been to Washington DC will not be surprised to learn that the Capitolio (Capitol Building) is an exact copy of the US capital's more famous building. It was ordered by Gerardo Machado, one of the most unsavoury of Cuba's list of dictators. Built in the 1920s, it took 5,000 workers over three years to complete and cost $17 million. Entry is through bronze doors whose reliefs represent stages in Cuban history to 1929. Machado's face was destroyed by a mob in the revolution of 1933. Inside, the sumptuous decoration is breathtaking, as is the vast bronze statue of an Amerindian woman representing Cuba. The 24-carat diamond set below the vast dome is the point from which all distances from Havana are measured.

CASA DE ÁFRICA ✪✪

33C3
Calle Obrapía 157
615798
Tue–Sat 10:30–5:30
Few
Cheap

This interesting museum and study centre explores Cuba's African heritage and has a collection of African artefacts. There is also the very interesting collection by Fernando Ortíz, a Cuban ethnographer, tracing the origins and beliefs of the Santería cult.

Opposite the museum is **Casa de la Obra Pía**, once the home of Alejo Carpentier, Cuba's finest 20th-century writer, who died in 1980. The house has some memorabilia (though Carpentier spent much of his life in Paris) but is chiefly worthwhile for itself, being one of Havana's finest 17th-century buildings. It is also one of the few that retains its slave quarters, on the roof.

Casa de la Obra Pía
33C3
Calle Obrapía 158
861 3097
Tue–Sat 10:30–5:30, Sun 9:30–12:30
Few Cheap

CASA DEL ÁRABE ✪

33D3
Calle Oficios 114
861 5868
Tue–Sun 9:30–6:30
None
Free

The beautiful 18th-century Colegio San Ambrosio is now a small museum of Islamic culture, with a collection mostly of gifts to Cuba from visiting Muslim leaders and diplomats, though there are also objects from Spanish/Moorish times. There is a small mosque – the only centre for Islamic worship on the island – and a rather good restaurant specialising in Middle Eastern food.

CASA NATAL DE JOSÉ MARTÍ (BIRTHPLACE OF JOSÉ MARTÍ)

José Martí, the father of Cuban independence, was born in Havana of Spanish parents in 1853. His Havana birthplace is now a museum to his memory, with writings and memorabilia that trace his life. Critical of Spanish colonial rule from his time at school, Martí was imprisoned for treason in 1870, and deported to Spain soon after. Although allowed to return to Cuba after the First War of Independence ended, he was soon arrested and deported again. Finally, in 1895, together with Maximo Gómez, Antonio Máceo and a handful of others, he landed near Baracoa to launch the Second War of Independence, only to be killed early in the war. He is buried at Santiago de Cuba.

➕ 32B1
✉ Calle Leonor Pérez 314
☎ 861 3778
🕐 Tue–Sat 10–5, Sun 9–1
🚌 Buses 232 and 264
♿ None
💷 Cheap

Above: *The main hall of the Capitolio Nacional is a masterpiece of space and light*

📌 33D4
✉ Plaza de Armas
☎ 861 6130
🕐 Daily 9–7
🍴 Coffee shop on site (£)
♿ Few 🚻 Cheap

CASTILLO DE LA REAL FUERZA ⭕⭕

The first fortress on this site was criticised for being ill positioned, a fact French pirates proved conclusively when they destroyed it in 1555. Nevertheless, the Castle of the Royal Force was rebuilt, though after its completion in 1577 it was made redundant by the better-sited fortresses

La Giraldilla

of Cabaña and El Morro (➤ 48). It then became the residence of the Cuban captains general (governors). Today the fortress, still impressively belligerent, its 3m-thick wall rising beyond a moat, houses a collection of modern ceramic work, exhibitions by contemporary Cuban artists, and a reasonable coffee shop with good views of the harbour. The *castillo* is also famous for La Giraldilla, the bronze figure of a woman above the westernmost tower. The most usual story says she is Doña Ines de Bobadilla, wife of Hernando de Boto, a 16th-century governor of Cuba who left to seek the Fountain of Youth and never came back. She spent every day for the next 10 years watching for his return. The figure – actually a replica, the original being in the City Museum (➤ 43) – is something of a symbol in Cuba and can be seen on many souvenirs, everything from postcards to rum bottle labels.

CATEDRAL DE LA HABANA (➤ 16, TOP TEN)

EDIFICIO BACARDÍ (BACARDÍ BUILDING) ⭕

📌 32B3
✉ Calle Monserrate esq San Juan de Oios (Progresso)

One of the best views of Havana is from the bar on top of the Hotel Plaza near Parque Central (➤ 42), but dominating the view is a much nearer building. Built in 1929 by the sugar and rum baron Emilio Bacardí, the Edificio Bacardí is an extraordinary piece of art deco architecture. Decorated with terracotta and (almost) naked nymphs, and topped by a giant version of the company's black bat, the building can certainly claim to be one of the most distinctive in the city.

One of the most distinctive façades in Havana, the Partagás cigar factory

FÁBRICA DE TABACOS PARTAGÁS

There are half a dozen cigar factories in Havana, but only the Partagás (near the Capitolio) and the **La Corona** (near the Museum of the Revolution) factories offer guided tours. To the disappointment of many visitors, cigars are rolled on wooden blocks rather than on the thighs of beautiful girls. Visitors are greeted by the rollers tapping their knives on their tables. A good cigar is made from four leaves: an inner leaf, then the flavour leaf, the combustion leaf that creates an even burn and the outer wrapper, which is glued with rice-glue. The ends are trimmed and, two minutes after starting work on it, the cigar is finished. The factories employ a reader for the rollers, an idea from the earliest days of production to ease the boredom of the work. José Martí was energetic in his efforts to get his anti-colonial pamphlets read at the factories, though romantic novels seemed (and are still) most popular. The La Corona factory produces Romeo y Julieta and Cohiba (Castro's favourite brand before he gave up after a 'heroic struggle'), but the Partagás factory has the better prices.

- 32A2
- ✉ Calle Industria 520
- ☎ 862 0086
- 🕐 Factory tours Mon–Fri at 10, 1; Shop Mon–Sat 9–5
- 🚌 Buses 232 and 264
- ♿ None
- 💷 Expensive (shop free)

Fábrica de Tabacos La Corona
- 32B4
- ✉ Calle Zulueta 106 e/ Refugio y Colón
- ☎ 862 0001
- 🕐 Factory tour and shop Mon–Sat 9–5
- 🚌 Buses 232 and 264
- ♿ None
- 💷 Expensive (shop free)

GRAN TEATRO

The Gran Teatro de la Habana claims to be the oldest theatre in the Americas, with a history dating back to 1846 when it opened (as the Teatro Tacón) with a Verdi opera. The claim is more or less true, the Tacón having been bought by a group of Galicians early this century and incorporated into the present structure, a superb art nouveau building. The theatre is home to Alicia Alonso's Ballet Nacional de Cuba, as well as offering regular performances of plays and classical concerts.

- 32A3
- ✉ Paseo de Martí (Prado)
- ☎ 861 3078
- 🕐 Tue–Sun 10–7
- 🍴 La Zaragozana (££), Avenida de Bélgica e/ Obispo y Obapría
- 🚌 Buses 232 and 264
- ♿ None
- 💷 Cheap

33C3
Calle Obispo 153
860 9529
Room 511 open Mon–Sat 10–5

HOTEL AMBOS MUNDOS

An absolute must for those on the 'Hemingway Trail'. When Hemingway first moved to Havana he stayed here, in Room 511. The hotel was his home, on and off, until he moved to Finca la Vigía. It is likely that it was here that he wrote the bulk of *For Whom the Bell Tolls*, his classic novel of the Spanish Civil War. The hotel, whose name means 'Both Worlds', was built as the elegant mansion of an 18th-century nobleman, though it was enlarged when it became a hotel. For many years the hotel was left to decay, but a full-scale restoration has been completed, making it one of the best hotels in the old town, its lounge a cool place to relax. Room 511 can be viewed: it is claimed to be as Hemingway left it, but has obviously had to be restored like the rest of the building, though the typewriter, model of the *Pilar* and empty whisky bottle are all probably authentic.

Hemingway (left) met Castro only once – at the annual marlin fishing tournament in 1960; the talk was of fish, not politics

33C1
Calle Cuba esq Acosta
Buses 232 and 264

IGLESIA DEL ESPÍRITU SANTO

The original church on this site was built in the 1630s, which has led to the present, larger church that incorporates it being called the oldest in Havana. A Moorish influence is still apparent. The first church was built by freed black slaves but an interesting sidelight on Cuba's social structure in the 17th century shows that burials – like life – were conducted here on a wealth basis. With grave sites at a premium, the wealthy could buy plots in the nave: those closest to the altar cost most. It is unlikely that any of the ex-slave builders could afford to be buried here. Inside the church there is a statue of St Barbara, equivalent to the god of thunder in the Santería cult.

IGLESIA DE SAN FRANCISCO DE ASÍS ✪
(CHURCH OF ST FRANCIS OF ASSISI)

The earliest church here was built in 1608 (pre-dating that of the Holy Spirit), but the present baroque building is much later. The church was a Franciscan monastery, but was later deconsecrated. It is now used for concerts. The church's tower was once the tallest in the city and was used as a landmark by approaching ships – and as a lookout in case the ships were pirates.

✚ 33D2
✉ Calle Oficios
🍴 La Torre de Marfil (£), Calle Mercaderes 111; Cafe el Mercurio (£) or Cafe del Oriente (£), Calle Oficios; Cafe Habana (£) nearby on Mercaderes
🚌 Buses 232 and 264

LA BODEGUITA DEL MEDIO ✪✪✪

Just a short step from the Plaza de la Catedral, though rather a longer one from the Hotel Ambos Mundos, is one of Ernest Hemingway's favourite bars. Legend has it that the bar started as a grocery store where writers met at lunchtime. The owner started to serve drinks, then meals... Opened as a full-time bar in 1942, the BDM (as the bar is colloquially known) has a décor that is unique and part of its great charm. The walls, ceiling and even the tables are covered in graffiti. The famous names inscribed here include those of such disparate characters as Errol Flynn and Fidel Castro. Pride of place goes to the framed words of Hemingway, 'My mojito in La Bodeguita, my daiquiri in El Floridita'. There are those who claim the text is a forgery, an invention by owners anxious to increase trade, but the forgery claim is itself dubious.

✚ 33C4
✉ Calle Empedrado 207
☎ 867 1375
🕐 Daily 10:30AM–1AM

Enjoy a mojito at La Bodeguita del Medio

Above: the boat that brought Fidel Castro to Cuba – now lovingly restored

MEMORIAL *GRANMA* ⭐⭐

The motor boat *Granma*, one of the most potent symbols of the revolution, is displayed adjacent to the Museo de la Revolución (➤ 22) and can only be viewed at close quarters by visiting the museum. After the failed attack on the Moncada barracks (➤ 88), Fidel Castro was captured (rather than shot as Batista had apparently demanded). He was tried and imprisoned on the Island of Youth (➤ 64), but released after two years and sent into exile in Mexico. There he was joined by his brother Raúl, Che Guevara and 79 fellow revolutionaries. In December 1956 they bought the motor boat *Granma*, an 18m vessel named by its Texan owner after his grandmother. The 82 rebels packed into the boat and after a storm-tossed crossing during which they were thrown well off course, they landed on Cuba's southeastern coast. Spotted from the air, strafed before they landed and pursued by troops, only a dozen revolutionaries made it to the Sierra Maestra mountains, from where these few launched the successful overthrow of Batista's regime. Today the *Granma*, neatly but vividly painted, is a national treasure. It is surrounded by other hardware of the revolution – vehicles from the Moncada raid and remnants of a US plane shot down at the Bay of Pigs.

MUSEO DE AUTOMÓVIL ⭐⭐

Many wealthy Cubans left the island in the wake of the revolution, taking their money, their clothes, and much else besides in some cases, but not their cars. The result was that Cuba – unable to import cars because of the American blockade and with economic ties to the USSR where cars were scarce – became a museum of 1950s US vehicles. Until just a few years ago the whole country, but especially Havana, was a delight for the classic car enthusiast, a procession of Buicks and Pontiacs – even Cadillacs

– cruising the city, kept alive by creative use of spares, remarkable feats of welding, and blind faith. Lately the government has realised the potential of these cars, persuading their owners to swap them for new Ladas (or, now, new Nissans) and selling them for huge prices to overseas collectors. Ironically, many (by devious means) return to the US. Havana's streets are now less of a classic car museum although there are still plenty on the roads; real enthusiasts need to visit this delightful little museum where they will find pristine versions of real classics, with other vintage models.

Classic cars are now rarer on the streets of Havana

MUSEO NACIONAL DE BELLAS ARTES (NATIONAL FINE ARTS MUSEUM) ✪✪

Housed in a 1950s building of interesting shape (a trapezoid), the National Fine Arts Museum has benefited greatly from a recent remodelling showing the works in an atmosphere and setting which allows their full appreciation. Here you'll find the finest collection of Cuban art on the island, together with some surprising works by European masters.

The ground floor is reserved for temporary exhibitions. The European paintings occupy the first floor and include works by artists such as Gainsborough, Turner, Rubens and Canaletto. The second floor is devoted to Cuban art, chiefly from the 20th century though there are some works by colonial artists. The 20th-century artists include René Portocarrero, with a style reminiscent of Chagall, and Wilfredo Lam, perhaps the Cuban painter best known to outsiders.

🗺 32B4
✉ Calle Trocadero e/ Zulueta y Monserrate
☎ 863 9042
🚌 Buses 232 and 264

MUSEO NACIONAL DE LA MÚSICA (NATIONAL MUSIC MUSEUM) ✪✪✪

This is the place for anyone with an interest in Cuban music, particularly its development from the African music of the island's slaves. The collection of instruments includes rare African drums, together with instruments that span the centuries from European colonisation to the present. There is a collection of sheet music, and numerous recordings which can be both heard and bought. The museum is also the venue for concerts: an events timetable is posted on the outside wall.

🗺 32B4
✉ Capdevila 1
☎ 861 9046
🕐 Mon–Sat 9–4:45
🚌 Buses 232 and 264
♿ None
💷 Cheap

MUSEO DE LA REVOLUCIÓN (► 22, TOP TEN)

41

➕ 32A3
✉ Paseo de Martí (Prado)
🍴 La Zaragozana (££),
Avenida de Bélgica
e/ Obispo y Obapría
🚌 Buses 232 and 264

*José Martí (below) called
for independence from
Spain from the Hotel
Inglaterra (bottom)*

PARQUE CENTRAL ✪✪

This park was the centre of the new Havana designed and, in part, constructed during the brief period when Cuba was under British rule. Later, after the Prado (➤ 43) was constructed, the park became the centre of Cuban life. To an extent it still is, though young Cubans have migrated towards the sea. At the park's centre, standing beneath tall palm trees, is a statue of José Martí, the first such memorial to have been erected in Cuba. It was paid for by public subscription and 'unveiled' in the presence of Maximo Gómez, another of the leaders of the Second War of Independence. Martí looks east towards the Supreme Justice Court and Manzana de Gómez, a department store built in 1910. At the time of its construction, and for many years after, it was the finest store in the Americas. Now it is occupied by a few unimpressive dollar shops.

Behind Martí is the Hotel Inglaterra, with a beautiful 19th-century classical façade. Now renovated, the hotel is justifiably popular with tourists. Beside the hotel is the Gran Teatro (➤ 37). Finally, at the northeastern corner of the park is the Hotel Plaza, an excellent hotel with fabulous views of the old town from its top-floor bar.

PASEO DE MARTÍ (EL PRADO) ✪✪

In the late 18th century a new promenade was laid out parallel to the old city walls, its form – and original name – mirroring the Prado of Madrid. Following the revolution, the promenade (about 1km in length) was renamed the Paseo de Martí though most Habaneros still use the old name. Few buildings on the street are open to visitors, but the whole offers a delightful stroll from Parque Central to the start of the Malecón. On the way, look out for the Palacio de los Matrimonios (No 302), once a casino and now a venue for weddings. Further on, to the right, is the Hotel Sevilla (a short distance along Calle Trocadero) made famous by Graham Greene in *Our Man in Havana*. The area has recently been renovated.

✚ 32A4
🍴 La Zaragozana (££),
Avenida de Bélgica
e/ Obispo y Obapría
🚌 Buses 232 and 264

Below: *the sumptuous Palacio de los Capitanes Generales echoes the lavish lifestyle of Cuba's Spanish governors*

PLAZA DE ARMAS ✪✪✪

This is Havana's oldest square, and one of the city's finest. A ceiba (silk cotton) tree marks the spot where a mass was held at the founding of the city, and near by is El Templete, a mock Grecian temple built in 1828 to commemorate the founding. The statue in the square is of Carlos Manual de Céspedes, instigator of the First War of Independence. On the northern side is the Castillo de la Real Fuerza (► 36), the Palacio de los Capitanes Generales, the palace of Cuba's colonial governors and its early presidents is to the western side. It is a beautiful building with elegant balconies and arcades; in the courtyard stands a statue of Christopher Columbus. The *palacio* now houses the **Museo de la Ciudad** (City Museum) displaying the original La Giraldilla from the Castillo de la Real Fuerza and other historical objects. As interesting as any item are the lavishly decorated rooms themselves. The (never used) Throne Room has a frescoed ceiling and gracious furnishings, while in the Hall of Mirrors, the eponymous mirrors are Venetian. Close by is the Palacio del Segundo Cabo, once the office of the vice-governor and now home to the Cuban Book Institute. On the southern side of the square is the Museo de Ciencias Naturales (Natural History Museum) with its (somewhat tired) collection of Cuba's extraordinary range of flora and fauna.

✚ 33D3
🍴 Café at Castillo de la Real Fuerza (£)
♿ None

Museo de la Ciudad
✚ 33D3
✉ Palacio de los Capitanes Generales, Plaza de Armas
☎ 861 5779
🕐 Daily 9:30–6:30
♿ Few
🖐 Moderate

The colonial-style courtyard of the Museo de Arte Colonial

🚏 33C4
🍴 La Mina (£££), corner of Plaza de Armas and Obispo

Centro Wilfredo Lam
🚏 33C4
✉ Plaza de la Catedral
☎ 861 2096
🕐 Mon–Sat 10–5
♿ None
💷 Cheap

Museo de la Educación
🚏 33C4
✉ Plaza de la Catedral
🕐 Mon–Sat 8–12, 1–5
💷 Free

Museo de Arte Colonial
🚏 33C3
✉ Plaza de la Catedral
☎ 862 2440
🕐 Tue–Sat 10–5:30, Sun 9–12:30
♿ Few
💷 Cheap

PLAZA DE LA CATEDRAL ⭐⭐⭐

The cathedral (➤ 16) dominates the square, but is not the only building of interest here. Close to it the **Centro Wilfredo Lam** has galleries of work by not only Lam, but contemporary Cuban and even some foreign artists. On the other side of the cathedral, in the northeastern corner of the square, the Casa de Lombillo, a beautiful *palacio* built in the early 18th century for the Marqués de Lombillo, now houses the **Museo de la Educación** (Museum of Education) with displays charting Cuba's progress in mass education. The Casa del Marqués de Areos, beside the museum, was built at about the same time – another *palacio* for another marquis.

Across the square from the cathedral is the plaza's other major building, the Palacio de los Condes de Casa Bagana, begun in the late 17th century but rebuilt in about 1720. It is a magnificent building, with a central courtyard and, upstairs, wooden ceilings. Today it houses the **Museo de Arte Colonial** with a fine collection of furnishings and decorations, mainly European in origin, from Cuba's colonial past. The final side of the square is formed by the Casa del Marqués de Aguas Claras, an elegant building dating from the mid-18th century, which now houses the El Patio restaurant.

A souvenir market with an abundance of stalls selling books, T-shirts, art and craft work can be found at Tacon, a block south of the Plaza de la Catedral.

Around Old Havana

Try to start in the early morning so that the sun makes the most of the important buildings along the way.

From the southwestern corner of Plaza de la Catedral (▶ 44), go along Calle San Ignacio, turning first left into Calle O'Reilly and continuing to the northwestern corner of Plaza de Armas (▶ 43). Turn right along the square's western edge, then right again along Calle Obispo (▶ 31). Go first left along Calle Mercaderes, passing the Hotel Ambos Mundos (▶ 38) and Casa de la Obra Pía, to reach the statue of Simon Bolivar.

The bronze statue was raised to commemorate one of the most famous of Latin American liberators.

Continue along Calle Mercaderes, passing Casa de África (▶ 34) and the Bolivar Museum (No 160). At Calle Brasil, turn right to Plaza Vieja. Cross to the bottom right corner and turn right along Calle Muralla. Go first left along Calle Cuba to see the restored Convento de Santa Clara.

The church and convent of Santa Clara, founded in 1638, is now the headquarters of the team restoring Old Havana. The delightful cloisters can be visited.

Return along Calle Cuba, and follow it northwards, crossing Calle Brasil to reach the Museo Histórico de la Ciencia Carlos J Finlay, on the left.

Carlos Finlay discovered that mosquitoes carried yellow fever, and the original site of the Cuban Academy of Sciences was named in his honour. The lecture theatre and a 19th-century pharmacy can be visited.

Continue along Calle Cuba, turning fourth right along Calle Obispo, then first left along Calle San Ignacio to return to Plaza de la Catedral.

Distance
3km

Time
1 hour's walking, at least 2 more for sightseeing

Start/end point
Plaza de la Catedral
✚ 33C4

Lunch
La Mina (£££)
✉ Corner of Plaza de Armas and Obispo

Convento de Santa Clara
✚ 33C2
✉ Calle Cuba
☎ 866 9327
🕐 Mon–Fri 9–3
💵 Cheap

Museo Histórico de la Ciencia Carlos J Finlay
✚ 33C3
✉ Calle Cuba e/ Amargura y Brasil
🕐 Mon–Sat 8–5
🍴 La Torre de Marfil (£), Calle Mercaderes 111
♿ Few
💵 Cheap

A game of dominoes in progress in Plaza Vieja

45

What to See around Havana

ACUARIO NACIONAL ✪

Although a little run down, the aquarium still shows visitors the huge diversity of sea life to be found off Cuba's shores. There are also dolphins who perform the usual tricks at regular intervals. Celia Guevara, youngest daughter of Che Guevara, is a vet here.

🕂 32A4
✉ Avenida 1 esq Calle 60
☎ 230 6401
🕐 Tue–Sun 10–6
💷 Cheap

CEMENTERIO DE COLÓN
(COLUMBUS CEMETERY)

A cemetery seems an unlikely tourist destination, but the Columbus Cemetery is extraordinary – a vast array of ornate sepulchres and gleaming, eye-achingly white sculpture. The tomb of José Raul Capablanca, Cuba's world chess champion, is topped by a large chess piece. One of the many legends about the cemetery concerns La Milagrosa (the Miracle Worker), Amelia Goyre de la Hoz, who died in still-born childbirth in 1901. One version has her husband visiting daily, knocking on the grave to announce his arrival, and holding conversations with her. People saw the ritual, and that his business went from strength to strength. In a second version, when the grave was opened the child buried at the mother's feet was in her arms. On the tomb a woman cradles a child in one arm and grasps a cross with the other. Habaneros come to knock on the grave, ask Amelia for help, then back away. Near by is an array of stones with flowers and messages of gratitude.

🕂 Off map
✉ Calle 23 (La Rampa)
🕐 daily, 7–6
🚌 Buses 67 and 264
♿ Few
💷 Cheap

The 'Miracle Worker's' tomb in the Columbus Cemetery is a place of pilgrimage

Guanabacoa's museum is one of the best in Cuba for exploring the Santería cult

GUANABACOA ✪✪

Now almost a suburb of Havana, Guanabacoa has still maintained its character. It is an old town, not only an early Spanish foundation but a thriving Indian settlement before that. The town's position made it a centre for the slave trade: Calle Amargua – Bitterness Street – is so-called because slaves were marched along it. There are one or two beautiful churches, but the main interest lies in the **Museo Histórico**, in a fine colonial mansion, which has the best collection on Afro-Cuban cults on the island, including Santería and the minor cults of Regla de Palo (which originated in the Congo and has strong links with Haitian Voodoo) and Abakuá (primarily a white Cuban cult and similar to the Freemasons). The Casa de Cultura is a centre for preserving Cuba's African heritage and there are frequent performances of traditional music and dance.

✚ 28B3

Museo Histórico

✉ Calle Martí 108 e/ San Antonio e Versalles

☎ 979117

🕐 Mon, Wed–Sat 10:30–6, Sun 9–1

🚌 Buses 3, 5, 105, 195 and 295

♿ None

🍴 Cheap

Did you know?

José Raúl Capablanca, born in 1888, was world chess champion from 1921 to 1927 and one of the greatest players of all time. Legend has it that the young Capablanca watched his father playing a friend and announced, after watching several games, that he wanted to play. His amused father set the board up and was promptly demolished by the boy.

32A4
Calle 21 esq O
873 3564

Above: *La Cabaña was once the largest fort in the Americas*

La Cabaña
33D5
On the western side of Havana's harbour
Daily 9–10
The bicycle bus through the tunnel under the harbour
None
Moderate

El Morro
33C5
On the western side of Havana's harbour
Daily 9–8
The bicycle bus through the tunnel under the harbour
None
Moderate

HOTEL NACIONAL

One of Cuba's most famous hotels, the twin-towered Nacional has been visited by such diverse characters as Winston Churchill and Marlon Brando. In the 1950s it was the site of one of Meyer Lansky's casinos. It fell on hard times, but was renovated in the early 1990s and is again one of the capital's most luxurious hotels. The downstairs bar has an interesting collection of photos of celebrities who have stayed here

LA CABAÑA AND EL MORRO

Although the Cabaña fortress – the Fortaleza de San Carlos de la Cabaña, to give its correct name – is the largest fort on the eastern side of Havana's harbour, it was not the first. That was El Morro, to the north, which was built over a 40-year period from 1589 with the twin objectives of protecting the harbour entrance and holding the high ground that dominated Havana. When the British attacked Cuba in 1762 they took El Morro and showed that control of the high ground was indeed critical: Havana fell soon after. When the Spanish regained Cuba they built Cabaña, arming the inland side of the fortress. This was the side from which the English had attacked as all its guns faced the sea. It accommodated 5,000 soldiers.

Each fortress has a small museum, including one of Che Guevara's time as commander at La Cabaña, and there is a lighthouse at El Morro with a great view. Cabaña is home to one of Cuba's most appealing traditions. At 9PM soldiers in 19th-century uniforms fire a cannon. In colonial times this told locals the city gates were about to close.

THE MALECÓN (➤ 20–21, TOP TEN)

MARINA HEMINGWAY ☻

Ernest Hemingway had no connection with this marina, set beside Avenida 5 (a continuation of the Malecón and usually just called Quinta by Habaneros) on the western edge of Miramar. It is, however, the centre for an annual marlin fishing tournament, held in May, and is an excellent base for watersports, deep sea fishing and diving. It also has a couple of restaurants called Papa's and Fiesta, maintaining the illusion that Hemingway had something to do with the site, but this is an expensive place to eat.

🔲 32A4
✉ Avenida 5 esq Calle 248, Barlovento
🍴 Papa's Restaurant (££); Pizza Nova (££), for the best pizza in Cuba!
♿ None

MUSEO DE ARTES DECORATIVAS (MUSEUM OF DECORATIVE ARTS) ☻☻☻

The Museum of Decorative Arts, housed in a palatial mansion, is the best museum outside Old Havana. Although furnished by Jansens of Paris, the furnishings are not just French but come from many European countries, while the woodwork is Cuban mahogany. There are marble-lined walls, Venetian glass, Wedgwood china and Meissen porcelain, furniture inlaid with mother-of-pearl,

hand-woven carpets, and a marvellous art deco bathroom in stunning pink.

🔲 32A4
✉ Calle 17, 502 e/ D y E
☎ 830 9848
🕐 Wed–Sun 10–5
🚌 Buses 67 or 264, Metro bus M6
♿ None
🎫 Moderate

Left: the Decorative Arts Museum is a homage to the furnishings of the late colonial period

MUSEO HEMINGWAY ☻☻☻

A little way south of Guanabacoa, in the hilltop village of San Francisco de Paula, is La Finca Vigía (Lookout Farm, so named for the military observation post that once topped the hill). The farmhouse, set in 9 hectares of gardens, was Ernest Hemingway's home for 20 years; it was given to the Cuban government after his death and is now the Museo Hemingway. Thefts by souvenir hunters have caused the closure of the house, but visitors can still view the rooms through the windows (open on dry days, closed on damp ones to preserve the contents). You can see the room where Hemingway worked, sometimes standing in front of the typewriter, for six hours daily. At Finca Vigía he wrote *The Old Man and the Sea* and his most controversial book, *Across the River and into the Trees*. In the grounds is the *Pilar*, the boat the writer sailed from Cojímar (▶ 17).

🔲 28B3
✉ San Francisco de Paula
☎ 910809
🕐 Mon–Sat 9–4, Sun 9–12 Closed Tue and rainy days
🚌 Metro bus M7
♿ None
🎫 Moderate

*All the anti-Castro plots
are laid bare here, at the
Museo del Ministerio del
Interior*

🕂 32A4
✉ Avenida 5 esq Calle 14
🕐 Tue–Sat 9–5
🚌 9 or 420
♿ Few
💰 Cheap

MUSEO DEL MINISTERIO DEL INTERIOR ⭐⭐

This extraordinary museum has a collection of exhibits allegedly obtained when various CIA plots against Castro or Cuba were foiled, and another collection dealing with the bravery of the counter-espionage agents. While the items from Cuban agents are gruesomely real, including bloodstained clothing, the collection of captured objects seems almost laughable. Stories have always been told of the CIA's assassination attempts on Castro, and hilarious tales of exploding cigars made it all seem more like boys at play than international intrigue. Confronted by a soap dish full of plastic explosive, you realise that many stories must have had a basis in truth, and that the players did indeed have a great deal in common with schoolboys – until you remember the bloodstained shirts.

🕂 32A3
✉ Calle San Miguel 1159
  esq Ronda
☎ 879 1412
🕐 Daily (except Mon)
  10–5:30 (closes at 12:30
  on Sun)
🚌 67 or 264
♿ Few
💰 Cheap

MUSEO NAPOLEÓNICO ⭐

Cuba is almost the last place you would expect to find a museum about Napoleon Bonaparte, but the collection is surprisingly good. Bonaparte's last doctor was a Corsican called Francesco, who retired to Cuba and died in Cienfuegos. The doctor's collection of memorabilia was acquired by a rich Habanero and installed in his Italianate mansion. The collection includes the hat Napoleon wore during his exile on St Helena, and a pair of pistols he carried at Borodino.

PABELLÓN PARA LA MAQUETA DE LA CAPITAL (HAVANA PAVILION) ★★

This modern (or post-modern) pavilion contains a scale model of Havana, a most interesting feature that allows a better understanding of the development of the city. At the other end of the road, away from the sea, a left turn leads to a delightful park shaded by huge banyan trees.

🏠 32A2
✉ Calle 28, 113 e/ 1 y 3
🕐 Tue–Sat 9:30–5:30
🚌 9 or 420
♿ Few
💷 Moderate

PLAZA DE LA REVOLUCIÓN ★★

The Plaza is used for national rallies, at many of which Fidel Castro is present, although he rarely addresses the crowd. It is also home to a huge (and, frankly, ugly) obelisk, a monument to the revolution. At its base is a white marble statue of José Martí, itself large, but completely dwarfed by the obelisk. Until very recently guards ushered away anyone careless enough to get too close to the statue and monument, but a small museum to Martí is now open at the base of the obelisk. Inside, you can take the lift to the lookout platform at the top and a stupendous view of the city. Behind the obelisk is the building in which Fidel Castro works. The leader is a very private man and few know where he lives. On the square's northern side the Ministry of Defence building bears a vast outline rendering of the famous portrait of Che Guevera, complete with the Revolutionary slogan *Hasta la Victoria Siempre* (Ever Onward to Victory). Next door, the Ministry of Communications building has a Postal Museum, which will be of interest to philatelists.

🏠 32A2
🚌 Buses 232 and 264

Memorial José Martí
🕐 Mon–Sat 9–5
💷 Moderate

This vast metalwork Che Guevera adorns the Plaza de la Revolución

✚ 32A4
✉ Calle 72, 4504
☎ 267 1717
🕐 Tue–Sun, doors open at
   8PM, show begins at
   10PM
♿ None
💷 Expensive

TROPICANA CABARET

The world-famous Tropicana is oddly sited at the edge of the Ciudad Libertad school complex (a former military airfield), some way from the centre of Havana. Here, in past days, appeared Maurice Chevalier, Carmen Miranda and Nat 'King' Cole, among others. It has been operating more or less continuously since its first night in 1931 and the show has changed little. This is no place for feminists, the long-legged, scantily clad mulatta girls being a clear link with another age. The show, performed beneath the stars, is not cheap, but worth considering just for the fun of it.

✚ 32A3
✉ Calle San Lázaro
🕐 Museums open Mon–Fri
   9–12 and 1–4
🍴 Bulerías (£), Calle L e/ 23
   y 25
🚌 Buses 67 and 264
♿ Few
💷 Cheap

Havana University

UNIVERSIDAD DE LA HABANA (HAVANA UNIVERSITY)

Close to the Hotel Habana Libre (once the Hilton) is the fine open campus of the University of Havana, founded by monks in 1728. The campus is a peaceful place after the hectic streets of Havana, and also has two small, but interesting, museums. The Natural History Museum, Cuba's oldest museum, has a good collection of the island's flora and fauna, while the Montané Anthropological Museum has a fine collection of pre-Columbian artefacts.

Southwards from Havana

Head eastwards along the Malecón, going through the tunnel that links the eastern and western sides of Havana's harbour, and continuing along Via Monumental. You will pass the fortresses of El Morro and La Cabaña (► 48). Continue along the main highway (which soon becomes the Primer Anillo de La Habana). The exit after the interchange with the Autopista Nacional (Carretera Central) allows a short detour into Santa María del Rosario.

The church in Santa María del Rosario is one of Cuba's finest colonial churches, with several baroque altars and some lovely late 18th-century murals.

Beyond the next exit from the main road is Avenida San Francisco at an angled T-junction near Parque Lenin. Turn left, then first right along Cortina de la Presa. The Las Ruinas restaurant is about 2.5km on.

Parque Lenin has hundreds of hectares of tree-scattered parkland around a lake with a golf course, swimming pool, horse-riding centre and zoo.

Continue along Cortina de la Presa to reach its T-junction with Carretera del Rocio. Turn right for 1.5km to reach the Jardin Botánico Nacional (National Botanical Garden).

Although suffering a little from neglect, the garden is still a fine place, especially for its collection of native trees and shrubs, and the lovely Japanese collection.

Reverse the route back to Avenida San Francisco and bear left along the main highway to reach its T-junction with the Avenida de la Independencia (traffic lights). Turn right and follow the main road to Plaza de la Revolución. Bear right at the Y-junction just before the Plaza, then turn left at the major interchange beside the Castilla del Principe. Follow the road (Avenida de los Presidentes) to the Malecón.

Distance
80km

Time
5 hours including stops

Start/end point
The Malecón, Havana
🚇 32A5

Las Ruinas restaurant in Parque Lenin

Lunch
Las Ruinas (£££)
✉ Cortina de la Presa, Parque Lenin
☎ 443026

Jardin Botánico Nacional
🚇 off map
✉ Carretera del Rocio
☎ 459159
🕐 Wed–Sun 8:30–4:45
♿ None
🔆 Moderate

53

Western Cuba

The western end of the island is the area of greatest contrasts, offering the most unspoilt landscape and the most modern, as well as the most characteristic.

The Zapata Peninsula is the last great wilderness on Cuba. Here there are species not only unique to Cuba, but unique to this swampland, a natural site of world importance. Yet it can be reached on a day trip from Varadero, the tourist centre of Cuba, where modern resort hotels line the white sands of the Atlantic shore. Close by is Havana, while to the west of the capital, on the long peninsula that reaches out towards the Yucatan Peninsula, are the fields where the finest tobacco grows. Kipling's famed comparison may be too chauvinistic for the end of the 20th century, but it still speaks volumes for Cuba's attitude to its most famous export. His poem *The Betrothed* was written after a famous 1885 breach of promise case, in which a young lady claimed her betrothed had broken off their engagement when she demanded he should choose between her and his habit of smoking Havana cigars.

> *'And a woman is only*
> *a woman, but a good*
> *cigar is a smoke.'*

RUDYARD KIPLING
The Betrothed

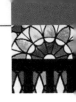

Matanzas

Originally sandwiched between two rivers, the Yumurí and the San Juan, Matanzas has now grown into a sizeable industrial city and port. After its foundation in the latter part of the 17th century, the city quickly became a major port for reprovisioning ships en route to Spain. The name, which derives from 'slaughter', may be a reminder of the herds of pigs and cows brought to the town, slaughtered and loaded on to the ships. A more sinister legend suggests that the slaughtered were people, perhaps Spaniards killed by Indians or (much more likely) Indians killed by the encroaching colonists. The town is backed by a mountain called 'Sleeping Beauty' by the locals as it is thought to look like a reclining pregnant woman. The drive past the mountain and along the coast towards Havana is one of the best on Cuba, with wonderful views of the Yumurí valley, particularly at Bayacunyagua, Cuba's highest viaduct, where turkey vultures can be seen soaring above the valley.

Today Matanzas is a slightly faded place, but its old centre is still worth visiting. Sadly, too many visitors staying at nearby Varadero ignore the town, sampling only the undoubted delights of Havana and Varadero itself. Yet here, just a short distance from the peninsula, is the real Cuba.

Looking towards the mogotes of Viñales, to the north of Pinar del Río

What to See in Matanzas

CASTILLO DEL MORRILLO

On the road from Matanzas to Varadero, just beyond the University, the Río Conímar flows into Matanzas Bay. At the river mouth stands an early 18th-century castle that is now a museum to Antonio Guiteras Holmes, a student leader executed in 1935 by Batista for forming a revolutionary group. Holmes and a fellow rebel were shot where the bronze busts of the pair now stand.

28B3
7km west of Matanzas
Tue–Sun 9–5
None
Cheap

CATEDRAL DE SAN CARLOS BORROMEO ✪

It is odd to find a Spanish cathedral in Cuba dedicated to an Italian saint. The 16th-century Cardinal Archbishop of Milan was, locals said, too ugly to be anything but a saint, but he was a tireless worker for Christianity. The late 19th-century building is on the site of a much earlier one destroyed by fire. Though in need of a good clean, the cathedral is still an impressive sight. Inside, the frescoed walls and ceilings are a delight.

28B3
Calle 83 esq 282
Café Atenas (£), Calle 83 esq 272

CUEVAS DE BELLAMAR (BELLAMAR CAVES) ✪✪

A regular destination from Varadero, these caves were allegedly found when a shepherd lost his dog (or sheep). They extend for about 2.5km (though only about 750m are open to the public) and have some beautiful limestone rock formations.

28B3
Finca La Alcancía, 6km southeast of Matanzas
Daily 8–5 (tours, lasting about 45 mins, start about every 30 mins)
There is a small café on site (£)
Not on a bus route. Join an organised tour from Varadero
None
Moderate

Parque Libertad is the centre of Matanzas' social scene

MUSEO FARMACEÚTICO ⭕⭕
(PHARMACEUTICAL MUSEUM)

Situated on the southern side of the Plaza de la Libertad, just a little way west of the cathedral, the Pharmaceutical Museum is housed in a pharmacy opened by a Frenchman in 1822. Almost all the jars and dishes, bottles, tools and recipes for producing all manner of ointments and potions have been preserved – absolutely fascinating.

✚ 28B3
✉ Plaza de la Libertad
☎ (052) 3179
🕐 Mon–Sat 10–5, Sun 10–2
🍴 Año 30 (£), Calle 272 e/ 75 y 77
♿ None
💷 Cheap

PALACIO JUNCO ⭕⭕

Close to the bay, this fine late 19th-century house of a plantation owner is now a museum to Matanzas' history. The museum includes a good section on slavery and the local sugar industry.

✚ 28B3
✉ Plaza de la Vigía
🍴 Café Atenas (£), Calle 83 esq 272

PLAZA DE LA VIGÍA ⭕⭕

The San Juan river is crossed by the Puente Calixto García, a movable steel structure erected in the last century. On its town side the bridge ends in this delightful square, where, on 1 January 1899, after the city had been bombarded by the US battleship *New York*, the Spanish surrendered to General Sanger of the US army. On the southern edge of the square the town fire brigade still occupies a fine neo-classical building dating from 1897. Inside there is an original fire engine. Opposite the station is a gallery showing the work of local artists.

✚ 28B3
🍴 Cafe Atenas (£), Calle 83 esq 272

TEATRO SAUTO ⭕

Across the road from the fire station is the town theatre, built by public subscription in the mid-19th century and one of the finest neo-classical buildings on the island. In its heyday it was the scene of glittering shows by some great artists, including Caruso and Anna Pavlova, and it still has a regular programme of events. If you are unable to catch a show, ask for a tour of the souvenir shop: it is worth while for the glorious paintings of the Muses on the ceiling.

✚ 28B3
✉ Plaza de la Vigía
🕐 Tue–Sat 9–12, 1–3
💷 Cheap

🏢 28C2

🚌 Daily buses from Jagüey Grande reach Playa Girón

Museo de Girón

✉ Playa Girón

☎ 535 4122

🕐 Daily 9–5

🍴 Villa Playa Girón has a reasonable restaurant (£) Cueva de los Pesces is a Cuban restaurant (££) and cafe (£) serving drinks and sandwiches

♿ Few

🎫 Cheap

What to See in Western Cuba

BAHÍA DE COCHINOS (BAY OF PIGS)   ⬤⬤⬤

Castro's nationalisation programme, and the forging of trade links with the communist world after the revolution, caused US antagonism towards Cuba to increase. Finally, in April 1961, a force of US-trained Cuban émigrés sailed from Florida and Guatemala to land at the Bay of Pigs. The Cuban Air Force attacked the invasion force's support ships, forcing them to withdraw as President Kennedy would not countenance direct intervention. Within three days, after several hundred had been killed, the beleaguered invasion force surrendered. One JFK murder conspiracy theory is that the Dallas shooting was orchestrated by exiled Cubans angry at the Bay of Pigs betrayal.

The Cubans name the invasion for the Bay's beach, Playa Girón, and a museum, **Museo de Girón**, at the village has a collection mainly of photographs and documents, but also including some captured weapons and a British-made Sea Fury fighter flown by the Cuban Air Force.

Most visitors come in search of the invasion, and many miss the bay itself. The crystal-clear sea is ideal for both diving and swimming – the whole eastern shore from Playa Larga to Playa Girón is a delight. The inlet is also famous for its sea life: sadly one aspect of this is unavoidable on the road along the eastern shore. In May and June thousands of crabs heedlessly cross the road (especially at dawn and dusk), and even the most careful of drivers will run over some of them.

At Cuevas de los Pesces you can hire flippers and snorkels to swim in an 80m deep submerged cave among jewel-like shoals of tropical fish.

The Bay of Pigs' warm, clear waters make it an ideal diving centre

Did you know ?

The Cuban flag was first raised in Cárdenas, when a band of several hundred men (largely American adventurers from New Orleans) landed here in 1850. When no local uprising followed, the men boarded a boat and sailed back to Florida. Not one shot had been fired.

CÁRDENAS ✪

Situated about 20km from Varadero, Cárdenas is a fine city, though in need of significant refurbishment. The city was not founded until 1828, which gives its centre a pleasing architectural wholeness. At the city's heart is the cathedral, most notable for the quality of its stained glass. The cathedral stands on the northern edge of Parque Colón, named for the statue of Christopher Columbus which was sculpted in 1862, making it the oldest of the great explorer in the Americas.

From the cathedral, head along Avenida Céspedes, going away from the sea, to reach Calle 12. Turn left here to reach a pair of good museums. The first is in the house in which student leader José Antonio Echeverría was born in 1932. Shot dead at the entrance of Havana University in 1957, he has become a national hero, and the **museum** has a collection of memorabilia about him, as well as a general historical collection.

Close to the Echeverría museum is the **Museo Oscar María de Rojas**, with an eclectic collection including butterflies, minerals, Amerindian objects, photographs, coins, weapons and an extraordinary 19th-century hearse.

A right turn at Calle 12 leads to Plaza Malakoff, the city's old market square. The Market Hall, built in the 1840s, is a remarkable two-storey iron construction in the shape of a cross with an iron dome 16m high.

✚ 28C3

Casa Natal José Antonio Echeverría (museum)
⊠ Calle 12 esq Avenida 4
☎ (05) 4919
🕐 Tue–Sat 8–4, Sun 8–12
🍴 Las Palmas (£), at Avenida Céspedes esq Calle 16 ☎ 054762
♿ None
💵 Free (but tip the guide)

Museo Oscar María de Rojas
⊠ Calle 12 e/ Avenida 4 y 6
☎ (05) 522417
🕐 Tue–Sat 9–5, Sun 8–12
♿ None
💵 Cheap

Christopher Columbus framed by the towers of the 15th-century cathedral in Cárdenas

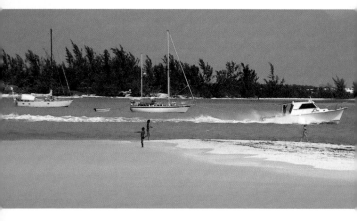

✚ 28B2

✉ 60km south of Zapata
Peninsula

✈ Regular flights from
Havana and Varadero

CAYO LARGO ⭐⭐

Around 1,600 islands and keys (shallow reef islands, from the Spanish *cayo*) surround Cuba. Cayo Largo lies south of the Zapata Peninsula, in the same archipelago (the Canarreos) as Cuba's largest island, Isla de la Juventud (➤ 64). It is about 27km long and 5km wide at its widest point, and is the island paradise of dreams – white sand surrounded by a clear, turquoise sea. Cayo Largo was a haunt of pirates in the 17th and 18th centuries, but until the early 1980s it had never been inhabited on a full-time basis. The government then decided to allow development up to a ceiling of 3,000 hotel rooms, a figure that present accommodation must be fast approaching. Most visitors are package tourists, but day or overnight trips are also available by air from Havana and Varadero.

Virtually the whole of the island's southern shore is beach, with the advantage of clean sand and warm water. Water sports are popular, as is wreck diving – the island's reefs have ensnared several ships in the past. Swimming can be dangerous because of an undertow and odd currents: watch for the red flags on the beaches. The eastern end of the island, the aptly named Playa Tortuga, is a nesting ground for sea turtles. Turtles can also be seen at a conservation hatchery at Combinado, the island's only 'town'. Here, too, there is a shop selling Santería-related artefacts, the only one in Cuba. From Combinado, boat trips are available to Cayo Iguana, a small island off Largo's western tip. The iguanas of the name are numerous and tame, but can also be seen on Cayo Largo. Cayo Rosario, an uninhabited island, can also be visited.

Cayo Largo is renowned for its clear sea and white sands; the best beach (above) is Playa Sirena

60

GUAMÁ AND LAGUNA DEL TESORO (TREASURE LAKE) ✪✪

The wildest parts of the Zapata Peninsula have already been described (➤ 26), but for the less intrepid there is much else to see on the peninsula. The Bay of Pigs and the beaches on its eastern shore (➤ 58) are the most obvious attraction, but Guamá and Laguna del Tesoro (Treasure Lake) are also worth visiting.

Villa Guamá was one of Fidel Castro's first ventures into tourism. Built across a dozen or so bridge-linked artificial islands in Treasure Lake, Guamá is a purpose-built tourist village with wooden huts in the style of Cuba's Amerindians.

At Boca de Guamá is the **Criadero de Crocodrilos,** where the native Cuban crocodile and its American counterpart are bred. The programme is in part a conservation exercise (for the Cuban species), but is also to supply skins for the handicrafts on sale, and meat for the restaurant. If you are tempted to buy, you must obtain a certificate from the shop or Cuban customs may confiscate the article: wild crocodiles are protected and poaching, though rare, does occur. Near the crocodile farm is a ceramics workshop where more ecologically sound souvenirs can be bought.

From the village, boats take you through a canal to the main lake (Laguna del Tesoro) to visit Villa Guamá. The lake is so called because of a legend that the local Amerindians, after bravely resisting the Spanish, threw their most treasured possessions into the lake rather than have them fall into Spanish hands. Their leader was called Guamá. Around the village are a number of wooden sculptures of Amerindians in a supposed reconstruction of native village life.

✚ 28C3

🍴 Villa Guamá (££)

🚌 Buses (3 times daily from Jagüey Grande to Playa Girón) pass the site

Criadero de Crocodrilos

✉ Boca de Guamá

🕐 Daily, 9–5

🍴 Villa Guamá (££)

♿ None

⚜ Moderate

The Villa Guamá, custom-built for tourists, stands beside the natural Treasure Lake

In the Know

If you only have a short time to visit Cuba, or would like to get a real flavour of the island, here are some ideas:

Young or old, Cubans are cigar smokers

10
Ways to Be a Local

Smoke a cigar. In restaurants and most public places, the smoke from numerous cigars will make abstainers feel like active rather than passive smokers, though smoking is now banned on public transport.

Rent a bicycle. The loss of Soviet oil in the early 1990s prompted Fidel Castro to try to transfrom the Cubans' love affair with the car to the bicycle. He succeeded.

Drive in a 1950s US car. There may be fewer around than 10 years ago, but you will still see classic cars, in various states of disrepair.

Smile. The Cubans are a happy people, with a smile never far from their faces.

Pick up a hitch-hiker. Inadequate public transport, low car owner-

ship and petrol rationing means that hitch-hikers are common. There are even official waiting/pick-up points. Be cautious (avoid young men), but picking up Cubans, perhaps an old couple, will make friends instantly.

Buy a guayabera. This loose-fitting pleated-front formal shirt is still the height of fashion for older Cubans on a night out.

Take an evening stroll. The *paseo* is part of the Spanish culture and is still followed by most Cubans.

Drink rum. Rum is the national drink and loving it seems to be compulsory.

Enjoy a leisurely lunch. Siesta is a Spanish word which should give you a clue. Relax, have a bite to eat, perhaps even a small drink. Then relax again.

Lap up the local music. Music is the lifeblood of Cuba: everywhere you go you will find bands playing. The mixture of Spanish and African roots has given

the Cubans both rhythm and style in their music.

10
Good Places to Have Lunch

Cafe El Mercurio
✉ Plaza San Fransisco, Old Havana. High ceilings, elegant, cool. Coffee and cakes or a full menu.

Casa del Árabe (£)
✉ Calle Oficios 12, Old Havana ☎ 861 5868. Specialises in Middle Eastern cooking in a beautiful colonial house dedicated to Cuba's Moorish past.

Casa Dos Gardenias (££)
✉ Avenida 7 esq 26, Havana Miramar ☎ 332553. Justifiably popular with tourist groups. Three different restaurants serve Chinese, Italian and Creole cooking. Try the Creole fried chicken with Moors and Christians and the coconut ice-cream.

La Isabelica (£)
✉ Calle Aguilera esq Porfirio Valiente, Santiago de Cuba ☎ (0226) 2230. The perfect place for a coffee and a quick bite during a tour of Santiago's historic centre.

La Terraza de Cojímar (££)
✉ Calle Real 161, Cojímar ☎ 653471. Eat *arroz con bacalao* (salt cod and rice) where Hemingway ate it.

Las Américas (££)
✉ Avenida Las Américas, Varadero ☎ (05) 667750 or 61612. Historically

interesting and with a wonderful view.

Las Ruinas (££)

✉ Cortina de la Presa, Parque Lenin, Havana ☎ 443026. In an old sugar mill in Havana's best park.

Mural of Prehistory (££)

✉ Viñales Valley. Another popular tourist restaurant (one without an official name, known only by its position), with visitors eating at long tables within sight of the mural. Good basic Creole cooking, usually with some Cuban vegetables to tempt the western palate.

Palacio de Valle (££)

✉ Calle 37, Cienfuegos ☎ (0432) 63666. Wonderful surroundings and great seafood.

Trinidad Colonial (££)

✉ Calle Maceo 402 esq Colón, Trinidad ☎ (0419) 2873. In a lovely old colonial house with a pleasant courtyard within 5 minutes' walk of the tourist centre. Good food –

Cuba's traffic-free roads are ideal for cyclists

international range, but with a Creole basis – in cool, elegant surroundings.

10 Top Activities

Baseball: a spectator sport seems an odd choice as an activity, but Cuban enthusiasm for the sport makes it an absorbing and breathless occasion.

Birdwatching: anywhere away from the towns will do, but the uplands (especially the Sierra Escambray and the Zapata Peninsula) are best.

Cycling: with so little traffic this is the ideal way of getting around.

Deep sea fishing: follow in Hemingway's wet footprints and hunt for marlin in the 'Blue Stream'.

Diving: all the resorts offer reef diving. On Cayo Largo there is excellent wreck diving.

Freshwater fishing: more relaxed and relaxing than its ocean cousin, but largemouth bass offer good sport.

Swimming/snorkelling: for those who cannot dive, much can be seen by snorkelling, and swimming in the island's warm waters.

Tennis: as might be expected, with its enviable climate Cuba is ideal for tennis. All the resort hotels have courts that can be hired, though there are no facilities in towns.

Walking: the lack of maps covering the island's wild areas can make this seem daunting, but with caution it will be rewarding.

Water sports: almost any

water sport can be followed in Cuba, from sailing to waterskiing.

5 Ernest Hemingway Sites

- Ambos Mundos Hotel, Room 511 (➤ 38)
- Cojímar (➤ 17)
- La Finca Vigía (➤ 49)
- La Bodeguita del Medio (➤ 39)
- El Floridita (➤ 102)

10 Rum Cocktails

- Cubanito – with tomato juice (the rum Bloody Mary)
- Cuba Bella – with crème de menthe, lemon juice and ice
- Cuba Libre – with cola and lemon or lime and ice
- Daiquiri – with lemon juice, sugar and crushed ice whisked together
- Havana Special – with pineapple and lemon juice, and ice
- Isla de Pinas – with vermouth and grapefruit juice
- Manhattan – with Angostura bitters, vermouth and plenty of ice
- Mojito – with lemon juice, sugar, mint and ice
- Piña Colada – with coconut cream and pineapple juice
- Saoco – a Piña Colada without the pineapple, which tastes best served in a coconut shell

Built by President Machado as an exact replica of Joliet Penitentiary, Illinois, the Presidio Modelo was Cuba's most feared prison

🕂 28B2
✈ By plane from Havana, several flights daily
🚢 Hydrofoil or ferry from Surgidero de Batabanó (hydrofoil twice daily, ferry on Wed, Fri and Sun)

Museo de Ciencias Naturales/Planetario
✉ Calle 41 esq 46, Nueva Gerona
☎ (061) 23143
🕐 Tue–Thu 8–7, Fri 2–10, Sat 1–5, Sun 9–1
🍽 Restaurante Dragon (£) Calle 39, near the church. Authentic Cuban and Chinese food
♿ Few
💷 Cheap

ISLA DE LA JUVENTUD ✪✪

Lying about 90km off the mainland's southern coast, Isla de la Juventud, the Island of Youth, is the largest of Cuba's offshore islands. The almost circular island is about 40km across. It was once favoured by pirates and reputedly called Treasure Island. There are many who believe Robert Louis Stevenson's *Treasure Island* was based on it: Stevenson never came here, but the topography of the real and fictional islands is very similar. It was named Island of Youth in 1978, when Cuba gave free education to thousands of young Africans here. Most of the island's population live on the north side; the southern shore – an almost continuous stretch of white sand with some of the world's best diving sites – is cut off by the huge Lanier marsh, which still harbours Cuban crocodiles (and large numbers of fearsome mosquitoes).

Nueva Gerona, the island's capital, with its rows of wooden houses, has several excellent museums (the best covers the island's natural history), a fine church and *El Pinero*, now beached as a memorial, which once ferried prisoners (including Fidel Castro) to and from the island. To

Once infamous as a prison island, the Island of Youth is now more famous for its college

the west of the town, the **Museo Finca El Abra** is where José Martí stayed during his imprisonment here.

The four five-storey, circular buildings of the **Presidio Modelo** used to house several thousand prisoners. It was here that Fidel Castro and the other prisoners of the Moncada attack (➤ 88) were brought. The prison is now, in part, a museum of its history.

In 1920 a ship-wrecked French sailor discovered the Caribbean's most important set of Amerindian pictographs and paintings in caves close to Punta del Este. There are over 200 in all, dating from as early as 1000 BC through to AD 800.

PENÍNSULA DE GUANAHACABIBES ✪

Beyond the town of Guane there are more fine beaches in the Bahía Corrientes. To the north, a freshwater lake – Laguna Grande – is famous for its fishing. Bahía Corrientes is excellent for diving, the local centre being at María la Gorda. This small resort – which translates literally as Mary the Fat – is named for a legendary Colombian woman kidnapped by pirates and installed in the bay to provide various services.

Beyond the bay the road enters the Guanahacabibes National Park, a UNESCO-backed biosphere reserve on the far western peninsula of Cuba. It was here that Cuba's Arawak Indians made their last stand against the Spanish invaders. Within the reserve wild pigs still roam on the low-lying limestone. The area is also important as a feeding stop for migrating birds.

Museo Finca El Abra
⊠ 3km southwest of Nueva Gerona
🕐 Tue–Sun 9–12, 1–5
♿ None
💷 Cheap

Presidio Modelo
⊠ 4km east of Nueva Gerona
🕐 Mon–Sat 8–4, Sun 8–1
♿ None
💷 Cheap

➕ 28A2
🚌 By taxi or tour bus only, no buses

Did you know ?

Tobacco plants for cigar production are planted as seeds in late October and take 2½–3 months to grow. The plants require continuous weeding and are very sensitive to climate. Just as with wine, Cuba's tobacco has vintage years – 1992 was superb – but cigars are rarely date-stamped. The leaves are harvested from the bottom upwards, the upper leaves taking longer to ripen but being stronger in flavour. After harvesting, the leaves are left to ferment before rolling begins. The fermentation reduces both the tar and nicotine content of the leaves, though these are already low in Cuban tobacco, an oddity of the soil.

PINAR DEL RÍO ✪✪

This very pretty town takes its name from the pines beside the Río Guamá. Its inhabitants are friendly and hospitable, despite being the butt of cruel jokes by the Habaneros. Pinar has always been a wealthy place, the local soil growing Cuba's best tobacco. Because of the town's economic importance, and the tourist potential of the nearby Viñales Valley (➤ 68), it was linked to Havana by an early *autopista*.

Entering the town from the *autopista* – which becomes Calle Martí, the main street, with an array of excellent neoclassical houses – the first place of interest is Palacio Guasch (c1910), to the left. A colonial mansion with a curious mixture of decoration – Greek columns, gothic spires and gargoyles, it now houses a **natural history museum**. Further on, also to the left, is the **Museo Provincial de Historia**, with memorabilia of Enrique Jorrín, credited with inventing the cha-cha-cha. At the centre of the town, the Teatro Milanés was built entirely of wood in the early 19th century. Beside it, the Museo Histórico de la Ciudad traces the development of the city and province of the same name. At the far end of Calle Martí, close to Plaza de la Independencia, is the town's only remaining **tobacco factory**. Here visitors can watch the hand-rolling of cigars.

VARADERO PENINSULA (➤ 25, TOP TEN)

✚ 28A3

Museo de Ciencias Naturales (Museum of Natural History)
✉ José Manti No 62
☎ (082) 3087
🕐 Tue–Sat 9–4:30, Sun 8–11:30
🍴 La Casona (£), Calle Martí – opposite Teatro Milanés
♿ None
💰 Cheap

Museo Provincial de Historia (Provincial Museum)
✉ Calle Martí 58
☎ (082) 4300
🕐 Mon, Wed–Sat 8–4, Sun 9–1
♿ None
💰 Cheap

Fábrica de Tabacos
✉ Calle Máceo 157, Plaza de la Independencia
☎ (082) 3424
🕐 Mon–Fri 7:30–4:30, Sat 7:30–11:30
♿ None
💰 Moderate

The best Cuban cigars are still made by hand

Around Pinar del Río

From the theatre, head west towards Plaza de la Independencia, turning first left along Calle Isabel Rubio. Follow the road across three crossroads, the first of which is slightly offset, and continue on to the Casa Garay liqueur factory.

Pinar is famous for the production of *guayabita*, a potent liqueur made by adding to rum the fruit of the name – a small, wild version of the guava, looking much like a rose hip – and a collection of herbs and spices. The factory (Fábrica de Bebidas Casa Garay) is now the only place in town where it is made. A shop at the factory sells the liqueur which comes in two forms: Guayabita Liqueur is amazingly sweet, while Guayabita Seca is mouth-puckeringly dry. Local wisdom has it that each is made more palatable by adding water.

Retrace your steps from the factory, turn first left and walk down to Calle Gerardo Medina. Turn right here to reach the Catedral de San Rosario.

The neo-classical cathedral, a somewhat dull building, was built in the late 19th century.

Turn left along Calle Antonio Máceo, crossing Calle Ormoni Arenado, to reach the birthplace of Antonio Guiteras Holmes, on the right.

Holmes, a 1930s revolutionary, was executed in 1935 near Matanzas. The house is now a small museum to him.

Cross Calle Rafael Morales and continue towards Plaza de la Independencia. The cigar factory (► 66) is to the left. Within the square there is an interesting shop selling local arts and crafts. Bear right across the square and turn right into Calle Martí, following it back to the theatre.

Picturesque buildings in Calle Máceo

Distance
2.5 km

Time
1½ hours, plus at least 2 hours for sightseeing

Start/End point
Teatro Milanés on Calle Martí
✠ 28A3

Lunch
La Casona (£)
✉ Calle Martí, opposite Teatro Milanés

Fábrica de Bebidas Casa Garay
✠ 28A3
✉ Calle Isabel Rubio 189
☎ (082) 2966
🕐 Mon–Fri 8:30–4:30
♿ None
🖐 Cheap

Museo Antonio Guiteras Holmes
✠ 28A3
✉ Calle Máceo 52
🕐 Mon–Fri 8:30–5, Sat 8:30–12
♿ None
🖐 Cheap

28A3

Casa de Don Tomas (£),
Viñales

By taxi or tour bus only,
no buses

Cueva del Indio

Viñales Valley, north of
Viñales

Daily 9–5

None on site, but the
Cueva San Miguel, closer
to Viñales, has a bar. In
the evening in the cave is a
cabaret/disco

None

Cheap

VIÑALES

The Viñales Valley is disarmingly beautiful and peaceful,
and equally interesting from a geographical point of view.
In the Jurassic era the area was topped by a limestone
sheet that was eaten away by the rainwater seeping into
crevices in the rock. Vast caverns formed, their roofs
supported by huge columns of rock that was slightly more
resistant to the water. In time the roofs collapsed, leaving
the columns behind. Erosion turned the roof rubble to a
rich soil and flattened the columns, creating *mogotes*, flat-
topped stumps of rock that exist in only a handful of places
on earth.

Viñales, the town of the valley, is as pretty as the
surrounding country, with rows of neat, freshly painted
houses shaded by pine trees, and a fine colonial church.
Much of the surrounding land is planted with tobacco.
From Viñales you can visit the **Cueva del Indio**, about 5km
north along the main valley road, a cave once inhabited by
Amerindians, where important artefacts were discovered.
Visitors can travel through the cave on foot and then by
boat across a narrow underground lake. To the west of
Viñales is the Mogote Dos Hermanos (Two Brothers
Mogote), on which the Cuban artist Leovigildo González, a
student of Diego Rivera, painted (at Castro's request) a
mural of man's evolutionary journey from amoeba to
Homo sapiens. The garishly coloured mural owes more to
enthusiasm than artistic skill, and the message is hard to
unravel, but it is an impressive undertaking.

28A2

about 20km southwest of
Pinar del Río

VUELTA ABAJO

West of Pinar del Río the hills fall away and the land
becomes increasingly marshy. This region, around San
Juan y Martinez, is known as Vuelta Abajo, and is almost
exclusively given over to tobacco growing. It produces the
best tobacco on the island, and tours of some of the
plantations are available.

Further west is the Bahía de Cortéz, a large and
beautiful bay. There is little development here and beaches
such as Playa Ballén, with a minimum of facilities, are
ideal for those seeking an entirely natural Cuba.

Above: *oxen still pull the
ploughs in the tobacco
fields of the Viñales Valley*

Through Western Cuba

This long but worthwhile drive will take a full day. An early start is recommended.

From Havana, head south from Plaza de la Revolución to reach the start of the Havana–Pinar del Río autopista. Follow it towards Pinar. After about 90km leave the autopista at the exit for Soroa and drive to this exquisite town high in the Sierra del Rosario.

The Soroa Valley has a plant life so exotic it is a registered UNESCO biosphere. A Spaniard from Lanzarote settled here in the 1940s and devoted himself to the growing of exotic plants. The resulting garden has a wonderful collection, particularly of orchids, with over 700 species, about 200 of them unique to Cuba. Many of the other plant species are also native to the island.

A rainbow often forms across the nearby waterfall, explaining why the Soroa Valley is sometimes called the Rainbow of Cuba. The intrepid can swim in the pool at the bottom of the falls.

Return to the autopista and continue to Pinar del Río (► 66). Here turn right just beyond Teatro Milanés (Calle Isabel Rubio/Carretería Central), then left, as signed – opposite the petrol station – for the Viñales Valley (► 68).

The quickest way back to Havana is to retrace the route along the *autopista*.

Alternatively, if time permits, follow the narrow, winding valley road that runs close to the north coast, a road with beautiful views of the sea through pine forests. Continue to Orlando Nodarse, then bear left for Mariel and the north coast autopista, which leads to Miramar and on to the Malecón.

Distance
350km

Time
8 hours including stops

Start/End point
Havana
✛ 28B3

Lunch
La Cabaña (£)
✉ Calle Martí, Pinar del Río
Aquita de Oro (£)
✉ Antonio Maceo esq Rafael Morales

Soroa Valley Garden
🕐 daily, 8–11:30, 1–3:30. Guided tours half-hourly
🍴 Villa Soroa
♿ None
💰 Moderate

The beautiful Soroa waterfall

Central Cuba

To the east of Varadero and the Zapata Peninsula lies the agricultural heart of Cuba. Here grows enough sugar to sweeten all the coffee cups in the world. The sugar fields – along with the coffee, the rice, and all the fruits and vegetables of the area – are tended by the *guajiros*, Cuba's farmers. In the evening the *guajiro* puts on his *guayabera*, the shirt that is now a fashion souvenir for Cuba's visitors, but during the day you will see him in a plainer shirt, loose-fitting trousers and a straw hat to keep off the sun. This is also the land of the cattle ranch and the *vaquero*, the Cuban cowboy.

Here too is Trinidad, the most famous village on the island. Remedios, though less well known, is almost Trinidad's equal; Santa Clara is where Che Guevara fought the battle that won the revolutionary war, while from the heights of the Escambray Mountains the view of the Caribbean is incomparable.

> *'It is clean, prosperous and quickly increasing.'*
>
> ANTHONY TROLLOPE
> (on Cienfuegos)
> *The West Indies and the Spanish Main*, 1859

———————•———————

The church in Sancti Spíritus is one of the oldest in Cuba

Cienfuegos

The Jagua Castle (▶ 73) protected the narrow entrance to Cienfuegos' vast harbour from the mid-18th century, but the town itself was not founded until 1819. Louis Clouet, a Frenchman, persuaded the Cuban Governor General to allocate land to people from Louisiana, which the US had just bought from France. Governor Cienfuegos agreed, and each of the new settlers was allocated a parcel of land by the harbour. In thanks, the settlers named their new town after him.

Soon Cienfuegos had become one of Cuba's major ports, its wealth reflected in the rows of buildings at the heart of the city, most of them in French neo-classical style. The huge natural harbour – it was claimed at the end of the 19th century that all the world's navies could safely anchor within its confines – ensured the city's continuing prosperity. After the revolution the Soviets moored submarines here, and poured in money to develop industries at the harbour fringe. Among other things, Cienfuegos boasts Cuba's biggest cement works and, to the southwest at Juraguá, its only nuclear power plant. Construction here began in 1980, but with the fall of the Soviet empire work stopped in 1992. The project was formally terminated by an agreement between Russia and Cuba in 2000.

Cienfuegos is famous for its colonial architecture

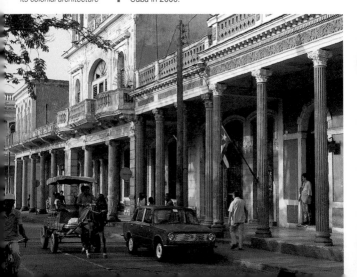

What to See in Cienfuegos

CASTILLO DE JAGUA ★★

The Castillo de Nuestra Señora de los Ángeles de Jagua (Castle of Our Lady of the Angels of Jagua) stands on the western approach to Cienfuegos' harbour. It was built at a time when the island had a thriving business relationship with pirates and privateers, and was under threat from the British. The castle is said to have been haunted by a lady in blue, reputedly the wife of a former governor of the castle.

One night, the story goes, a soldier attacked the ghost. Dawn found him completely insane, with blue cloth wrapped around his sword. The lady was never seen again.

PALACIO DE VALLE ★★

The exotic Palacio de Valle at the southern edge of the city is said to have been built by Moroccans at the request of a local industrialist, which explains the Moorish (though not the gothic) touches. Today it houses a very good restaurant and a small museum of furniture and porcelain.

PARQUE MARTÍ ★★

Any visit to Cienfuegos must start at Parque Martí, at the centre of the old town. On the park's eastern edge is the Catedral de la Purisima Concepción, a plain but dignified twin-towered building. Its treasure is a series of 12 windows, depicting the Apostles in French stained glass. On the square's northern side is the Teatro Tomás Terry, built by sons of a wealthy plantation owner of that name. Caruso is among the great stars to have performed here. Opposite the cathedral is the Palacio Ferrer, built for another sugar millionaire and now the Casa de la Cultura where concerts are held. The mansion's tower can be climbed for a fine view of the city. On the southern edge of the square stands the Museo Historicó, with a small collection exploring the city's history.

✚ 28C2
✉ At the western approach to Cienfuegos' harbour
🕐 Daily, 8–4
♿ None
💵 Cheap

Palacio Ferrer's impressive tower overlooks the city

✚ 28C2
✉ At the southern end of Calle 37 (Paseo del Prado), beside the Hotel Jagua
☎ (0432) 551226
🕐 Daily 8–4
🍴 Restaurant (££) in palace
♿ Few
💵 Cheap

✚ 28C2
🍴 El Palatino (£), Avenida 54, 2514 (on south side of the square)

73

What to See in Central Cuba

CIEGO DE AVILA ★

➕ 29D2

🍴 El Colonial (£), Calle Independencia 110

🚌 Tour buses from Havana and Varadero. Daily regular bus service from Camagüey and Santa Clara

Situated at the edge of a flat and low-lying rectangle of land, the town takes its name from its position, a *ciego* being the forested edge of a pampas (plain). The pampas here are at Cuba's narrowest point, a bottleneck between the island's mountainous central and eastern regions. During the First War of Independence, the Spanish created a defensive line across the area, from Morón, close to the Atlantic coast, to Júcaro on the Caribbean coast, a line pivoted around Ciego. The defences consisted of a 40km double fence with about 40 blockhouses. It proved too long to be held and was easily turned by the rebels. Undaunted, when the Second War of Independence broke out, the Spanish reformed the 'Trocha' ('short-cut path'), as the line was called, but again the rebels broke through.

Today the pampas beside Ciego are Cuba's most important fruit-growing area. The land is particularly good for pineapples, a type called Española Roja being especially sought after for export. Ciego de Avila is a market town for the fruit growers and local cattle breeders. It is a quiet, unassuming place, which offers a glimpse of the real urban Cuba. The Teatro Principal, a short distance from Parque Martí at the heart of the town has large, beautiful doors carved from local wood. Beside the park, with its monument to José Martí, is the fine old town hall. Elsewhere, there is a small museum with items on the revolution from a local perspective.

ESCAMBRAY MOUNTAINS (► 19, TOP TEN)

Two studies in the struggle for independence: portraits of Che Guevara (above) and Camilo Cienfuegos (right) in Ciego de Avila

Through the Escambray Mountains

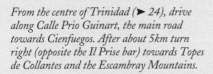

From the centre of Trinidad (➤ 24), drive along Calle Prio Guinart, the main road towards Cienfuegos. After about 5km turn right (opposite the Il Prise bar) towards Topes de Collantes and the Escambray Mountains.

The road to Topes de Collantes is stunning, the mountains rising quickly to over 930m. The hillsides are cloaked in forests, but where the trees have been cleared there are coffee plantations. Topes de Collantes was created as a health resort, today the hotel and spa complex is being heavily developed as an eco-tourism centre.

Beyond Topes, ignore a turning right to Lake Hanabanilla, continuing through the mountains.

The views towards the Caribbean (left), are stupendous, while soon, on the right, Pico San Juan, at 1,872m the highest peak of the Escambray, is reached.

The road descends to reach the main road just beyond the village of La Sierrita. The return journey from here depends upon time. Turn left for a direct return, passing close to several fine beaches. It is about 60km (1 hour) to Trinidad and lunch, a drive with wonderful views. If you have time, turn right towards Cienfuegos, soon going through the village of Arimao and on to San Antón.

The Soledad Botanical Gardens are about 5km further along the road (before the Karl Marx cement works, one of the most visible local landmarks).

Alternatively, a left turn from San Antón heads to Rancho Luna, a new resort with an excellent beach and good diving. After lunch, reverse the route back to the main road, turning right to follow it back to Trinidad.

Distance
190km

Time
6 hours

Start/End point
Trinidad
🗺 28C2

Lunch
Colonial Trinidad (££)
✉ Calle Máceo 402 esq Colón, Trinidad
☎ (0419) 2873
Hotel Rancho Luna (££)
✉ Playa Rancho Luna
☎ (0432) 5929 or 2951

Thatched-roofed old farms are dotted around the valleys of the Sierra del Escambray

➕ 29D2
🍴 Hotel Morón (££),
   Avenida de Tarafa
   ☎ (0335) 3408
🚌 Bus from Ciego de Avila

MORÓN ✪✪

This delightful small town was named after an Andalusian village by its original settlers from southern Spain. Locally it is known as the 'city of the cock' after a (probably legendary) gold cockerel that once stood in the centre of the town. The bird was stolen by pirates, but village pride eventually required that a cock should again adorn the centre and a bronze replacement was sculpted. The dictator Batista thought the occasion presented a useful photo opportunity and decided that he would perform the unveiling. Mysteriously the bird disappeared: rumour has it that the sculpture was melted down by rebels. Then in the 1980s a new cock was placed at the entrance to the town's hotel. At 6AM and 6PM an electronic crowing erupts from the adjacent clock tower, a surreal touch.

Morón is a pleasant, quiet town, a good centre for exploring the local north coast, an area popular with fishermen and hunters. The fishermen make for the Laguna de Leche, Milk Lake, a brackish lagoon with lime-based sediment, which, when disturbed, gives the milky look of the name. The lake is famous for its largemouth bass and tarpon. Bass can also be caught in the nearby Lago La Redonda, which is popular with wildfowlers.

Off the coast near Morón are the Camagüey Keys, a line of large islands. The most westerly, Cayo Coco, is now linked to the mainland by a 33km causeway and is being rapidly developed as a tourist centre.

Cayo Coco's 22km of palm-fringed sandy beaches make it an alluring holiday destination

REMEDIOS ✪✪✪

Remedios was founded in the early 16th century by Vasco Porcallo de Figueroa (who is said to have fathered over 200 children). Originally it stood on the coast, but frequent pirate raids forced townsfolk to move the settlement inland. Today it is one of the finest colonial towns on the island and famous as the venue for Cuba's most striking festival, the *Parrandas*. This started in the early 19th century when the local priest employed children to walk the streets on Christmas Eve, banging cans together to keep the population awake for Midnight Mass. Soon the two districts (*barrios*) of the town were competing with each other to create the loudest noise. Today they build vast floats called *trabajos de plaza*. Fireworks and lights flash from secret doors in the floats and the whole 'contest' is accompanied by ear-splitting music. The festival offers a memorable, if noisy and sleepless night. Those who miss it can catch the flavour at the **Museo de las Parrandas**, devoted to its history.

On the main square, the church of **San Juan Bautista** is claimed by many to be the loveliest in Cuba. The altar, carved wood embellished with gold leaf, is by the artist Rogelio Atá. It was the gift of a rich benefactor in 1939. Close by are two small museums, one exploring the town's history (at Calle Máceo 56). The other is the **Museo de Musica Alejandro García Caturla**. Though a lawyer by profession, Caturla was also a composer, whose influence on Cuban music was significant. His incorruptibility as a lawyer and his liberal views led to his murder in 1940, when he refused a leading politician's bribe.

Though not as well known as Trinidad, Remedios has an equally well-preserved colonial heart

✚ 28C3
🍴 Hotel Mascotte (£££),
Parque Martí ☎ (042)
395144

Museo de las Parrandas
✉ Calle Maximo Gómez 71
☎ (042) 395382
🕐 Tue–Sat 9–12, 1–5, Sun 9–1
♿ Few
💷 Cheap

Church of San Juan Bautista
✉ Calle Camilo Cienfuegos 20 (on Parque Martí)

Museo de Musica Alejandro García Caturla
✉ Parque Martí 5
☎ (042) 395382
🕐 Tue–Sat 9–12, 1–5, Sun 9–1
♿ None
💷 Cheap

✠ 29D2
🍴 Merendero el Puente (££)
beneath the bridge on
Jesus Menendez

Museo de Arte Colonial
☎ (041) 25455
✉ Calle Plácido Sur 74
🕐 Tue–Sat 8:30–5, Sun
8–12
🍴 Mesón de la Plaza (£),
Plaza Honorato
♿ None
💰 Cheap

SANCTI SPÍRITUS ⊙⊙

After a visit in 1895, Winston Churchill recalled Sancti Spíritus as 'a very second-rate place, and a most unhealthy place' (*My Early Life*). Since Churchill's visit, the health of the town and its inhabitants has improved immeasurably, and though it is not in the first rank of tourist destinations, Sancti Spíritus deserves better than 'second rate'.

The town was one of the original seven *villas* (garrison towns) set up by Diego Velázquez in 1515 (► 10), the only one that was truly inland. The *villa* was moved after a few years, to a site on the Yayabo river. Though far from the sea, it was raided by pirates (and sacked twice) in the mid-17th century. In the years of peace that followed, the fertile lands that surrounded the town – and which now form the province of which Sancti Spíritus is the capital – supported vast sugar plantations that made their owners, and the town, rich. Sugar is still the most important local crop. The cane feeds the country's biggest sugar mill, while the cane trash is used to produce paper in a mill almost as big.

At the heart of the city is Parque Central (also called Parque Serafín Sanchez after a hero of the two Wars of Independence, whose birthplace at Calle Céspedes 112 has been turned into a small museum in his honour). The town church, the Iglesia del Espíritu Santo, lies a little way south. Declared a National Monument in 1978, it was built in the late 17th century on the foundations of a wooden church of 1522, perhaps the oldest in Cuba. The church tower was added in the 18th century and the cupola some 100 years later. The carved ceiling is claimed by many to be the finest on the island.

Closer to the square is the **Museo de Arte Colonial**, housed in a perfectly preserved 19th-century colonial mansion built for the Valle Iznaga family, at the time the most important family in the area. The mansion, with its beautiful courtyard, is superb, its elegant design being complemented by the furniture

*Sancti Spíritus' cobbled
streets (top right) were
carefully restored in the
late 1980s, but the
Puente Yayabo (right)
remains as built*

and furnishings. The latter form one of Cuba's best collections and include paintings, glassware and ceramics. There is also a *tinajon*, a filter and storage jar used to turn suspect river or spring water into good drinking water. A larger version of the same sort of filter can be seen near the Yayabo bridge, positioned so that people entering the town could pause for a drink.

The Yayabo bridge is the only stone-arched bridge left on the island. The river it crosses has given its name to the *guayaba*, the wild version of the guava (used to make the famous guayabita liqueur at Pinar del Río ➤ 67) and the *guayabera*, the loose-fitting shirt that was developed by workers from the town. Near the river, Calle Llano, another National Monument, is a winding, cobbled street with a collection of exquisite 19th-century houses. The Teatro Principal, also close to the bridge, is home to the *Coro de Claro*, a local choir that has achieved world renown.

✚ 28C3
🍽 Hotel Santa Libre (£)

Tren Blindado
✉ Calle Independencia
☎ (0422) 2758
🕐 Tue–Sun 8–12, 2–6
♿ None
💷 Cheap

Museo Provincial Abel Santamaria
✉ Calle Esquerra
☎ (0422) 203041
🕐 Daily 8–12, 1–6 (closed Sat PM)
♿ Few
💷 Cheap

Hotel Central, in Santa Clara's Parque Vidal, has been beautifully restored

Museo Histórico de la Revolución
✉ Arenida Vidal
☎ (0422) 5593
🕐 Daily 8–5 (closes at 12 on Sun)
♿ None
💷 Cheap

SANTA CLARA ✪✪

Santa Clara is the capital of Villa Clara province – the most unspoilt of central Cuba's regions. The town was founded in the late 17th century by people who discovered that even the new inland village of Remedios (➤ 77) was not remote enough to ensure relief from pirate attack. Despite that early founding, Santa Clara does not have many rich colonial houses. It is, rather, a workmanlike place, though that does not imply dullness – more than most provincial capitals Santa Clara is busy, filled with a sense of urgency and purpose.

The town's position, almost at the heart of Cuba, has made it strategically important during the many battles for independence. Most famously, it was here that the decisive battle of the revolution was fought, with the victorious revolutionaries led by Che Guevara.

Ernesto Guevara achieved world fame because of the famous Alberto Korda photograph, shot at a rally in Havana, but his place in Cuban history was already secure: on 28 December 1958 his handful of rebels attacked Santa Clara. When Che's men bulldozed a trainload of supplies sent by Batista to his beleaguered troops, the dictator realised that Santa Clara was lost; he resigned and fled on 1 January 1959. The remaining troops at Santa Clara surrendered the same day.

There is much in Santa Clara that commemorates the battle. The **Tren Blindado** is easily the most extraordinary memorial: the derailed trucks of the train (and the bulldozer, mounted on a plinth) have been preserved; there is also a small museum. The barracks where Batista's men surrendered is now the **Museo Provincial Abel Santamaria**, exploring the battle and other aspects of Santa Clara's history, as well as the natural history of Villa Clara. In the Plaza de la Revolución is the **Museo Histórico de la Revolución**, with a mural of the battle and a massive statue of Che in battle dress, inscribed with that popular revolutionary slogan '*Hasta La Victoria Siempre*'– 'Ever Onwards to Victory'. And perhaps most significantly, there is the mausoleum inaugurated on 8 October 1997, when the bones of Che Guevara were brought back from Bolivia to rest in state at the site of his greatest triumph.

Did you know ?

Most books suggest that Ernesto Guevara was nicknamed 'Che' because it means 'pal' or 'mate' in Spanish, Guevara being a friendly guy. The truth is that in Argentinian speech it is inserted into sentences rather like 'you know' in English. The Cubans, unfamiliar with this, rapidly used the verbal hiccup to identify their Argentinian colleague.

Of non-revolution Santa Clara, the best part is Parque Vidal (named for another revolutionary, Leoncio Vidal, who died in an earlier battle at the town, in 1896). On the square's northern edge is the fine, yellow-walled Teatro La Caridad and, close by, the **Museo de Artes Decorativas**, with a collection of colonial furnishings. At the square's southwestern corner, the Hotel Libre maintains a bullet-marked façade, one more memorial to Che's battle.

TRINIDAD (▶ 24, TOP TEN)

Museo de Artes Decorativas
✉ Parque Vidal 27
☎ (0422) 205368
🕐 Mon 1–6, Wed–Thu 9–6, Fri–Sat 1–10, Sun 6–10
♿ None
💵 Cheap

The eastern edge of Parque Vidal

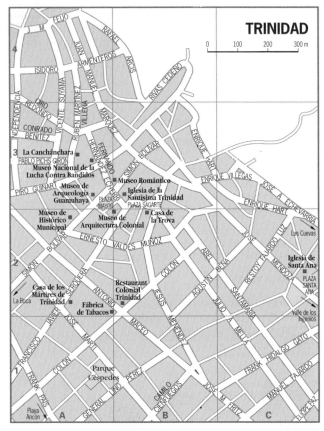

TRINIDAD

0   100   200   300 m

J. M. FEIJÓ
RAFAEL
JUAN ARMENTEROS
MANUEL
ARCIS
ISIDORO
VICENTE SUYAMA
RIVAS CEDEÑO
GIRO REDONDO
INDEPENDENCIA
CONRADO BENÍTEZ
RUBÉN MARTÍNEZ VILLENA
FERNANDO HERNÁNDEZ ECHERRI
MÁRQUEZ
ENRIQUE IBARI

3 La Canchánchara ■
PABLO PICHS GIRÓN
Museo Nacional de la
Lucha Contra Bandidos ■
PIRO GUINART
Museo de ■
Arqueología
Guanuhaya
SIMÓN BOLÍVAR
Museo Romántico ■
PLAZA MAYOR
Iglesia de la
Santísima Trinidad
PLAZA SAGARTE
ENRIQUE VILLEGAS
JOSÉ A. ECHEVARRÍA
ENRIQUE HART
Las Cuevas

Museo de ■
Histórico
Municipal
Museo de ■
Arquitectura Colonial
Casa de ■
la Trova
JOSÉ
RESTOY FAJARDO LUZ
MENDOZA

ERNESTO VALDÉS MUÑOZ

2
SIMÓN BOLÍVAR
SERIOLERA
COLÓN
ABEL
BENA
AGUSTÍN
SAN IAMARÍA
Iglesia de
Santa Ana
PLAZA
SANTA
ANA
Valle de los
Ingenios

La Boca
Casa de los ■
Mártires de
Trinidad
ANTONIO MACEO
JAVIER
Restaurant ■
Colonial
Trinidad
Fábrica ■
de Tabacos
JESÚS
MENÉNDEZ
JULIO A. MELLA
FRANK HIDALGO GATO
MANUEL FAJARDO

1
FRANCISCO
COLÓN
MARTÍ
FRANK PAÍS
Parque
Céspedes
GENERAL LINO
PÉREZ
CAMILO
CIENFUEGOS
JOSÉ M. FRUIZ
FELIPE PAZ

Playa
Ancón
A   **B**   **C**

*The Museo Romántico is
housed in an early 19th-
century* palacio

Around Trinidad

From the northern corner of the square, go along Calle Echerri, passing between the Museo de Arqueología Guamuhaya and the Museo Romántico (▶ 24). Turn first left into Calle Piro Guinart.

On the corner of Calle Piro Guinart is the Museo Nacional de la Lucha Contra Bandidos, in an old convent with a pretty bell-tower. The museum deals with the early 1960s struggle against counter-revolutionaries in the Escambray Mountains.

Walk along Calle Piro Guinart. The first turning right leads to La Canchanchara, a bar named after its famous cocktail, made from rum, honey and lemon. Ignore the first three turns to the left, then turn left along Calle José Martí, following it to the House of the Martyrs on the corner of Calle Zerquera.

Casa de los Mártires de Trinidad explores the lives and deaths of the 72 Trinidad residents who died during the revolution.

Continue along Calle Martí (a turn left along Calle Colón reaches a small cigar factory which can be toured) to reach Parque Céspedes, on the left. At the far end of the square, turn left along Calle Lino Pérez, following it across several intersections to reach the church of Santa Ana.

Only the shell of this fine church now remains. Close by, the old town prison has been converted into a gallery (Plaza Santa Ana) for local artists and craftspeople.

Return along Calle Pérez, turning second right along Calle Santamaria. When it ends at a T-junction, turn left (along Calle Values Muñoz), then first right to return to the Church of the Holy Trinity (▶ 24) and Plaza Mayor.

Distance
2.5km

Time
1 hour, plus another 2 hours for visits

Start/End point
Plaza Mayor
✚ 82A3

Lunch
El Jigüe (££)
✉ Calle Martínez Villena esq Piro Guinart
☎ (0419) 4315

Museo Nacional de la Lucha Contra Bandidos
✚ 82A3
✉ Calle Piro Guinart
☎ (0419) 4121
🕐 Tue–Sun 9–5
✋ Cheap

Elaborate wrought-iron grille

Eastern Cuba

The east is the revolutionary heart of Cuba. Here the first war for independence from Spain began; here Fidel Castro first led rebels against Batista's forces; and here, after his imprisonment and exile, Castro landed with Che Guevara to start the conflict that led to Batista's overthrow.

Castro and his men hid in the mountains of the Sierra Maestra, Cuba's highest peaks, a paradise for walkers who are experienced enough to travel well off the beaten track. Beyond the mountains is Santiago de Cuba, once the island's capital and now its second city, with a wonderful centre full of colonial buildings. On again is Guantánamo and the US Naval Base, a curious hangover of colonial rule. To the north is the coast where Columbus first landed in the New World. With its Amerindian sites and hidden colonial treasures, it is one of the most interesting areas of Cuba, and is still as beautiful as when Columbus first saw it.

> ' *[the] island is the most beautiful that eyes have ever seen* '
>
> CHRISTOPHER COLUMBUS
> From his diary of the journey to the New World, 1492, quoted by his son Hernando in *The Life of the Admiral*

Santiago de Cuba

One of the original seven Spanish settlements on Cuba, Santiago was soon made the island's capital, as its deep harbour was a natural base for the conquistadores. Santiago became a wealthy city, the discovery of copper in the hills to the west leading to rapid expansion. The city soon had to forfeit the status of capital to Havana, however, partly because of the pirate raids that followed the increase in prosperity – Henry Morgan even sacked the city after the Morro fortress had been built.

At the end of the 18th century the slave revolt in Haiti led to a massive influx of French plantation owners into Santiago. They brought with them their knowledge of sugar and coffee farming, and the rapid establishment of plantations led to a large number of slaves being shipped into Santiago. The French also brought their own culture, which, together with that of the African slaves, created one of Cuba's most cosmopolitan and exciting cities, best illustrated by Santiago's carnival. Banned until recently, the carnival (held in July) shows every sign of re-establishing itself as the island's most colourful event. Those unable to make it to the carnival can sample its various aspects at the **Museo del Carnaval**.

Santiago's position in Cuba's various independence conflicts was critical. The black general Antonio Máceo, known as the 'Bronze Titan' and a hero of both the Wars of Independence, was born in the city. And it was here that Castro made his first speech after Batista's flight, giving Santiago the title 'Hero City'.

What to See in Santiago de Cuba

CASTILLO DEL MORRO ✪✪✪

This dramatic castle at the entrance to the bay was built in the mid-17th century to stop pirate raids on Santiago. It is one of the finest viewpoints on the island, with superb vistas to the Sierra Maestra. The castle houses a museum of piracy, with sections on 'old piracy' (Henry Morgan et al) and 'new piracy' in the form of the CIA.

Museo del Carnaval
- ✚ 86B1
- ✉ Calle Heredia 302
- ☎ (0226) 626955
- ⏱ Tue–Fri 9–5, Sat 9–11, Sun 9–5
- ♿ None
- 💵 Cheap

Above: *Dominoes in Tivoli, the old French quarter near the Padre Pico steps*

- ✚ 29E1
- ✉ South of Santiago, near the airport
- ☎ (0226) 691569
- ⏱ Mon–Fri 9–5, Sat–Sun 8–4
- 💵 Cheap

SANTIAGO
DE CUBA

0   250 m

*Calle Bartolomé Masó,
close to Parque Céspedes*

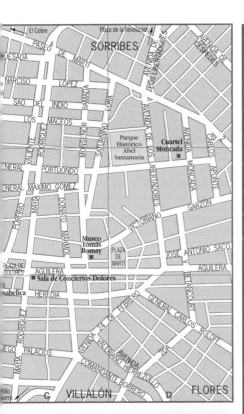

The well in the courtyard
of Casa de Velázquez

87D2
Avenida Moncada
(0226) 620157
Few
Cheap

Above: Cuba's struggle for independence is illustrated in the Moncada Barracks

29F1
20km west of Santiago
Taxi or tour bus only, no buses

Cafetal La Isabelica
Gran Piedra
(0226) 641517
Tue–Sun 8–3
None
Cheap

29F1
About 45km west of Santiago
By taxi or tour bus only, no buses

Valle de la Prehistoria
Parque Baconao
(0226) 639039
Daily 7–6:30
None
Cheap

CUARTEL MONCADA (MONCADA BARRACKS)

It was here on 26 July 1953 that Castro launched his first attack against Batista's forces. The early-morning raid was a miserable failure, with many rebels being killed (or captured and executed). Castro himself was afterwards imprisoned and later deported. Today the barracks, the bullet-holed façade lovingly tended, houses a school and a museum of the revolution.

GRAN PIEDRA

A beautiful road heads east from Santiago towards the southern coast. After about 10km a road to the left leads up the Gran Piedra (Big Rock, 1,220m), an outlier of the Sierra Maestra. Close to the peak is a hotel/restaurant. From here 440 steps lead to the summit, crowned by the vast lump of rock that gives it its name. On clear days you can see Haiti and Jamaica.

A short distance beyond the hotel is the **Cafetal La Isabelica**, the mansion of an old coffee plantation, now a museum of plantation life.

PARQUE BACONAO

The park covers an area of over 800sq km and includes a nature reserve, a hunting reserve, several good beaches and some interesting tourist sites. The latter include the **Valle de la Prehistoria**, with its collection of life-size concrete dinosaurs. Not far beyond is the Conjunto de Museos de la Punta, a series of fine museums (collections of cars, dolls, costumes, stamps and much more), and a shopping mall close by. To get there, take a left turn opposite one on the right for Daiquiri. Beyond the museums are the El Mundo de la Fantasia fun park and Acuario Baconao (➤ 111).

PARQUE CÉSPEDES (➤ 23, TOP TEN)

A Walk Around Santiago de Cuba

From the cathedral in Parque Céspedes (➤ 23), head west along Calle Heredia, then turn first left along Calle Félix Peña. Turn second right along Calle Diego Palacios to reach the top of the steps on Calle Padre Pico. On the hill behind you is the Museo de la Lucha Clandestina.

The museum tells the story of the urban guerillas who fought in the streets of Santiago during the revolution.

Walk down the steps and continue along Calle Pico to Calle Aguilera. Turn right, then first left. At the crossroads, turn right along Calle José Saco, Santiago's main shopping street (known as Enramadas).

Enramadas is fascinating, with its mix of dollar and peso shops.

Follow the street to the Plaza de Martí. The Museo Tomás Romay is on the left.

Museo Romay has collections on natural history and archaeology, and some modern paintings.

Turn right along the square's western edge, then right again, following Calle Aguilera to Plaza de Dolores. Continue along the square's left-hand edge, then turn first left (Calle Rosado), passing the Museo Bacardí on the right.

Museo Bacardí was founded by rum baron Emilio Bacardí. It contains collections of weapons and paintings.

At the next intersection, the Museo del Carnaval (➤ 85) is to the left. Turn right and follow Calle Heredia, soon passing the Casa Natal de José Heredia to the left.

José María de Heredia, born in Santiago in 1803, is regarded as one of Latin America's finest poets.

Continue along Calle Heredia to return to Parque Céspedes.

Distance
3km

Time
1½ hours; 4 hours with stops

Start/End point
Parque Céspedes
✚ 86B1

Lunch
La Isabelica (£)
✉ Calle Aguilera

The Museo de la Lucha Clandestina is housed in an attractively restored colonial building

Museo de la Lucha Clandestina
✉ Calle General Jesús Rabí 1 (top of Padre Pico steps)
🕐 Tue–Sun 9–5
♿ None
💰 Cheap

Museo Tomás Romay
✉ Calle José Saco esq Barnada
🕐 Tue–Sat 9–5, Sun 9–1
♿ None
💰 Cheap

What to See in Eastern Cuba

BARACOA

✚ 29F1
🍴 Restaurante Guamá (£),
    Fuerte de la Punta
☎ (021) 43335

In October 1492 Columbus landed on the northern coast of Cuba believing he had reached Japan. The exact place of his landing is still disputed – but not by the inhabitants of Baracoa. They have no doubt that Columbus came ashore here, pointing to their most treasured relic, the Cruz de la Parra, as proof. The cross, now in the church of Nuestra Señora de la Asunción in Plaza Indpendencia, is reputed to have been brought ashore by Columbus and planted on the beach. It was lost for many years, being found among vines (hence the name, the Cross of the Vines). Recently, carbon dating was carried out on the wood; it was found to date from the mid-15th century, Columbus' era.

Outside the church stands a statue of Hatuey, the chief of the Amerindians, who put up a strong fight after Diego Velázquez created the first permanent settlement at Baracoa in 1512. When Hatuey was captured Indian resistance ended. Today he is a hero to the Cubans, who see him as resisting imperialism. Despite the inscription which states that Hatuey's death was in Yara, Baracoa, he was actually executed in another Yara, near Manzanillo. The municipal museum in Fuerte Matachin, an 18th-century fort – one of three within the town's boundaries – has more on Baracoa's fascinating history .

Baracoa is a lovely place, although beginning to suffer from the growth of tourism. It has a couple of pleasant restaurants, and there are few better places on the island to relax.

The Casa de la Cultura is one of Baracoa's finest buildings

Did you know?

Christopher Columbus' diary of his journey to the New World notes that there was a flat-topped mountain close to his first landfall. Baracoans claim this to have been El Junque, on the western side of their bay. And they were not discouraged by the conclusion of an international conference of historians and geographers, in 1936, that Bariay Bay to the west was in fact the site of the first landing.

Below: *children enjoying a goat-cart ride in Bayamo*

BAYAMO ✪

Bayamo is the capital of the province of Granma, named after the boat that brought Castro, Guevara and the other 80 rebels to Cuba at the start of the revolution. Carlos Manuel de Céspedes, hero of Independence, was born in a house in the main square, now a museum devoted to him. His statue stands in the square (Parque Céspedes) and a plaque on the Ayuntamiento (Town Hall) recalls that here, in 1869, he signed a declaration abolishing slavery in 'Free Cuba'. Eventually forced from power in the free state by internal wranglings, Céspedes retired to nearby San Lorenzo to concentrate on his great passion, chess. Surprised by Spanish troops while contemplating a move at the board, he declined to surrender and was shot dead. Beside the **birthplace museum** is the **Museo Provincial**, with items on the town's history, including the original score of Cuba's national anthem written by local poet Perucho Figueredo, whose bust can also be seen in Parque Céspedes.

➕ 29E1

🍴 Restaurant 1513 (£), Calle General Garcia 176

Casa Natal de Carlos Manuel de Céspedes

✉ Calle Máceo 57 (on west side of Parque Céspedes)
☎ (023) 423864
🕐 Tue–Sun 9–5
♿ None
💵 Cheap

Museo Provincial

✉ Calle Máceo 55
☎ (023) 424125
🕐 Tue–Fri 8–6, Sat–Sun 10–2
♿ Few
💵 Cheap

🗓 29D2
🍴 La Compañía de Toledo
(£), Plaza San Juan de
Dios

Casa Natal de Ignacio Agramonte

✉ Avenida Agramonte 459,
near Plaza de los
Trabajadores

☎ (032) 297116

🕐 Tue–Wed 10–5, Thu–Fri
12–10, Sat 10–6, Sun
8–12

🍴 Pizzeria Ragazza (£), Calle
Máceo

👋 Cheap

CAMAGÜEY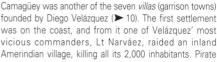

Camagüey was another of the seven *villas* (garrison towns) founded by Diego Velázquez (▶ 10). The first settlement was on the coast, and from it one of Velázquez' most vicious commanders, Lt Narváez, raided an inland Amerindian village, killing all its 2,000 inhabitants. Pirate attacks and mosquitoes forced the Spaniards to move inland. It is said that the new town occupied the old Indian village site and that the name Camagüey was the name of the slaughtered Indians' village.

The move failed to deter pirates, however: the town was sacked by Henry Morgan in 1668 and again ten years later by the French pirate François Granmont. But the townsfolk were determined to stay, the local land (now Camagüey Province) being good for both sugar and cattle. It is here that visitors are most likely to see *vaqueros*, Cuban cowboys.

Although Camagüey is Cuba's third largest city and has some fine colonial buildings, it is rarely visited by tourists. This explains both the poor state of some of its architectural gems and the pleasing lack of the usual hangers-on who attach themselves to tourist groups.

As you walk in the town you are bound to pass one of the terracotta vessels called *tinajones*. This area of Cuba being short of water, with few rivers and little rain, the townsfolk invented the *tinajon*, a huge pot into which the infrequent rainwater was guttered. When piped water made *tinajones* redundant, the art of their manufacture was lost, but it has recently been revived. A local legend has it that if a man drinks water offered to him by a woman from her *tinajon* he will stay with her in Camagüey for ever.

Waiting for fresh bread in Parque Agramonte

Not surprisingly for such a large city, Camagüey has its hero of the independence struggles. Ignacio Agramonte was born here in 1841 and led the local rebels during the First War of Independence. He was killed in 1873. His birthplace, the **Casa Natal de Ignacio Agramonte**, is a museum to him.

The first church on the site of the **Catedral de Nuestra Señora de la Candelaria**, in Parque Agramonte, was built in 1530. The present impressive building dates from the 19th century. It apparently contains some fine marble tombs (but was closed for restoration at time of writing).

Well north of the city centre, near the railway station, the **provincial museum** is housed in an old Spanish barracks. Its excellent collections include the history of the area, local natural history and colonial furnishings, plus a small collection of paintings and some excellent *tinajones*.

Plaza de los Trabajadores (Square of the Workers) is most notable for the lovely colonial church of **Nuestra Señora de la Merced**, a former convent church with a venerated image of the baby Jesus. The arched façade is delightful and inside are some superb 18th-century frescoes, thought by many to be the finest in Latin America. Lovers of churches should also visit the church of La Soledad, a short distance to the northeast.

About the same distance from the Plaza, but to the northwest, the Teatro Principal is an impressive building with excellent stained glass and crystal chandeliers.

Catedral de Nuestra Señora de la Candelaria

✉ Calle Cisneros esq Luaces (south side of Parque Agramonte)

🍴 La Compaña de Toledo (£), Plaza San Juan de Dios

Museo Provincial Ignacio Agramonte

✉ Avenida de los Mártires 2 esq Calle Ignacio Sánchez

☎ (032) 282425

🕐 Tue–Sat 9–5, Sun 8–12

♿ Few

💰 Cheap

Nuestra Señora de la Merced

✉ Plaza de los Trabajadores

🍴 Pizzeria Ragazza (£), Calle Máceo

Left: *the huge church of La Soledad houses some fine baroque frescoes*

93

Food & Drink

Traditional Cuban cuisine is an exciting blend of Spanish and African cooking, which can be difficult to find today, when economic restrictions mean that much of the island's produce is exported to earn foreign currency.

Drink in La Bodeguita del Medio (below) and eat in El Patio (bottom), both in Havana – the latter strictly for the ambience only

The food served at most tourist hotels is of the type usually labelled 'international', often described by the consumers as bland. Things are sometimes a little better in the state-run restaurants, and can be much better in the *paladares* (▶ 105, panel). These spring up and close down with a rapidity which defies the possibility of a list being compiled, but are worth seeking out.

Cocina Criolla

Cuba's *cocina criolla* (Creole kitchen) is a basic cuisine, built around providing nourishing food for agricultural workers. The basis will be meat (vegetarians are likely to be frequently disappointed in Cuba), usually pork, but occasionally chicken. Beef is rarely served (even in the tourist hotels), despite the herds of cattle travellers see in central Cuba. If beef is available it will be *picadillo* (minced) or *palomilla* (steak brushed with olive oil and garlic). Meat is usually roasted (*carne asada – puerco asado* is roast pork) or grilled and served with a mix of rice and beans –

called *congri* if the beans are kidney beans, or *moros y cristianos* (Moors and Christians, a jokey reference to the island's own racial mix) if they are black beans.

Rice and beans are also the basis of *potage*, usually served first, a filling mixture of white rice and a thick bean soup. Similar to potage is *ajiaco*, a thick peasant stew of meat and vegetables, usually heavily flavoured with garlic.

For vegetable you will probably be offered a poor seasonal salad, yuca or plantains. Yuca is a native root vegetable, similar to cassava, which is boiled or baked. Plantain is a cooking banana and is usually served as *maduros* or *tostones*. For *maduros* slightly sweeter plantains are lightly fried. *Tostones* is one of Cuba's specialities – plantains are cut into thick strips, fried, then flattened by hand and refried.

As for dessert, export means that very little of the usual Caribbean fruit finds its way to market and menu. But Cuban ice-cream (*helado*) is excellent. If it is not on the menu, look for the Coppelia ice-cream parlour – every town has one.

What to Drink

Cubans start the day with coffee. A *café Cubano* (also known as *cafecito* or *mezclado*) is served in a small cup and is very black and strong. The Cubans lessen the impact with heaped spoonfuls of sugar. After a meal it is better to go for a *café con leche*, that is 'with milk'. *Café americano* is the same thing.

Non-alcoholic drinks are in short supply, though occasionally fruit juices are available, as is *guarapo*, a sugar cane pressing.

All Cuban beers are lager. The most popular is Cristal, which is not as strong as Bucanero. Malty Polar, and Tinima from Camagüey are other popular brands.

For spirits drinkers, Cuba means rum (*ron*). It comes in 3-, 5- and 7-year (*tres, cinco* or *siete años*) forms, the youngest being the cheapest. Basic rum is 'white' (colourless), but can be made to darken by storing in oak barrels or the addition of caramel. Rum is also the basis of Cuba's numerous cocktails. The mojito and daiquiri are the most famous, but the Cubanito (a rum bloody Mary) and the Cuba Libre (rum and cola) are equally popular (➤ 63).

On the Rocks
A *mojito* is made from rum, soda water, lime juice, sugar and mint, a *daiquiri* from rum, sugar, lime and crushed ice, whisked to create the perfect cocktail. The latter has a much debated history. Did US troops find the locals making the drink when they landed at Daiquiri Beach during the Spanish-American War? Or was it invented by a miner at the Daiquiri copper mine near Santiago? The only certainty is that a real Cuban daiquiri is nothing like the cocktail you will buy elsewhere.

In Cuba all cocktails are rum cocktails

EL COBRE (▶ 18, TOP TEN)

GUANTÁNAMO ●●

The most scenic way to Guantánamo is the coast road from Santiago, but the main inland road is faster.

The US naval base, the reason most visitors have heard of Guantánamo, cannot be seen from the town, which has little of the colonial splendour of other Cuban towns: the far east of the island was always its poorest part, a mountainous, difficult area. But do spend time in Parque Martí, where the splendid town church stands, or visit the Zoologico de Piedra (Stone Zoo), where a local amateur sculptor has created stone animals, wholly from pictures.

To see the naval base it is necessary to go south of the town to Malones where an observation platform allows a view of the 'imperialists'. The base, on the two pincer-like horns enclosing Guantánamo Bay, was created in 1898 during the Spanish-American War, and was made permanent formally in 1901 as part of the grudging Cuban acceptance of the Platt Amendment. This gave the US the base in perpetuity. In 1934 The Amendment was abrogated in favour of a 99-year lease with an annual rent of $4,085. Each year the US sends a cheque which Castro declines to cash, maintaining that to do so would legitimise an illegal occupation. Since 2001, the base has housed detainees, essentially prisoners from the war in Afghanistan. Stories abound of Cubans swimming across the bay to the base, braving sharks, jellyfish and tides. After the rafters crisis of 1994 some 30,000 Cubans at the base were admitted into the US. Rioting over poor conditions and re-escapes back to Cuba led to immigration talks, and now officially all Cubans who reach the base are returned to Cuba.

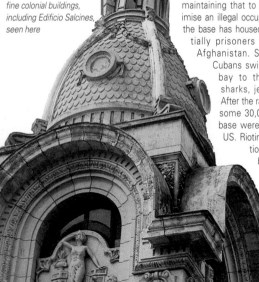

Guantánamo has some fine colonial buildings, including Edificio Salcines, seen here

From Santiago to Guantánamo

In Santiago, from the northern edge of Plaza de Martí, take Avenida Victoriano Garzón, continuing along Avenida Raul Pujol (past Santiago's Zoo, on the right). Avenida Pujol becomes the road to Parque Baconao which soon passes the Granjita Siboney, to the right.

Distance
220km

Time
8 hours

Start/end point
Santiago de Cuba
✠ 29F1

Lunch
Casa de Rolando (£)
✉ Laguna Baconao, Parque Baconao, to the east of Santiago de Cuba

The road to Granjita Siboney is lined with simple stone monuments to those killed at Moncada. It was at the farmhouse of Granjita Siboney that Castro and his men stayed the night before the disastrous attack on the Moncada Barracks (➤ 88).

At the village of Siboney, bear left for Parque Baconao (the road ahead leads to Playa Siboney, a fine beach). Follow the road for 10km to reach the Valle de la Prehistoria (➤ 88).

The road to Parque Baconao is a beautiful mix of semi-desert (complete with cacti), pasture, cane fields and forest. At Laguna Baconao there is a small crocodile farm and a pleasant restaurant overlooking the lake (a popular haunt of pelicans). The road to the lake passes the El Mundo de la Fantasia fun park and the Acuario Baconao (➤ 111).

Playa Cazanol, one of several fine beaches in Parque Baconao

Beyond Laguna Baconao the road becomes a dirt track, but with care this is easily driven (except after heavy rain) to reach tarmac again at a T-junction. Turn left and drive into Guantánamo (➤ 96). The road reaches the town on its western outskirts: turn left to follow the Carreteria Central past the bus station and on towards Santiago, or continue ahead to reach the autopista (beware of horse-drawn carts!), which soon reaches the Carreteria Central. Follow the main road (but using another section of autopista to cut off a long winding section) back into Santiago.

✚ 29E2

🍴 Mirador de Mayabe (£), on top of Loma de Mayabe, 10km southeast of the town

Museo de Historia Provincial

✉ Parque Calixto García

☎ (024) 463395

🕐 Mon–Sat 9–5

♿ None

🖑 Cheap

Museo de Ciencias Naturales

✉ Calle Máceo 129 e/ Martí y Luz Caballero

☎ (024) 423935

🕐 Mon–Fri 9–5, Sat 1–5

♿ None 🖑 Cheap

Above: the Parrot Cage is so called because of the red, green and yellow uniforms of the Spanish soldiers besieged there

HOLGUÍN   ❤❤❤

Cuba's fourth city is the capital of one of the island's most beautiful and richest provinces, with a prosperous sugar industry and nickel and cobalt mines in the mountains close to the town. Columbus probably landed here, and Angel Castro (Fidel's father) was one of the province's sugar farmers.

Holguín has a centre notable for the number of squares, the most important of which is Parque Calixto García, named for a local hero of the Wars of Independence. García's birthplace, a little way to the east, is now a museum dedicated to him. On the northern edge of the square, the **Museo de Historia Provincial** is housed in an old mansion used as barracks by the Spanish and known as La Periquera (the Parrot Cage) since the brightly uniformed Spaniards were besieged in it for two months by local insurgents during the First War of Independence. The museum has one of Cuba's best pre-Columbian collections, including the so-called Holguín Axe, an Amerindian stone axe carved in the shape of a man. The axe is the symbol of the province. Across the square is the **Museo de Ciencias Naturales**, a natural history museum with a collection including specimens of some rare Cuban birds and several thousand coloured shells of polymita snails, found only in eastern Cuba.

Close to Holguín the Loma de la Cruz (Hill of the Cross) is a place of pilgrimage following a vision of the Virgin in 1790. Pilgrims climb 468 steps, but visitors can use a road to reach the panoramic view from the summit. Another good viewpoint is the Mirador de Mayabe, topped by an Amerindian-style hotel/restaurant.

North of Holguín, at Bariay Bay near Gibara, a monument marks the spot where, it is believed, Columbus first landed in the Americas. To the east is the excellent, and rapidly developing, beach resort of Guardalavaca, which reputedly takes its name from the saying *guarda la vaca y guarda la barea* (watch the cow and watch the boat) – a reference to the locals' ancient habit of supplying fresh meat to passing pirate ships.

South of Guardalavaca, at Banes (where Fidel Castro was married in 1948) is the **Museo Indocubano**, one of Cuba's most important Amerindian museums. Some of the artefacts in the museum were excavated from the **Chorro de Maita** Taino Indian burial site, close by. Here you can see the corpses arranged exactly as they were when they were found, in 1986.

Museo Indocubano

✉ Calle General Marrero 305, Banes

🕐 Tue–Sat 9–5, Sun 8–12

♿ Few

💲 Cheap

Museo Chorro de Maita

✉ South of the village of Yaguajay

🕐 Tue–Sat 9–5, Sun 9–1

♿ None

💲 Cheap

The early 18th-century Church of San Isidoro dominates Parque Peralta

Did you know ?

On 2 December 1956 the Granma, *with its cargo of Fidel Castro, Che Guevara and 80 other revolutionaries, was blown off course by a storm, and landed on the edge of swampland at Playa Las Coloradas to the north of Cabo Cruz. Today the landing site is a sacred place in the history of the revolution.*

🚹 29E1
🍴 Restaurant 1800 (£), Calle Merchan 243

La Demajagua
✉ About 8km southwest of Manzanillo
🕐 Open at all reasonable times
♿ Good
🎫 Free

Mural of Columbus' arrival in the Casa de la Cultura

MANZANILLO ⭐

Manzanillo's position, separated from Santiago by the Sierra Maestra and a long way from Havana, helped it to become a favourite haunt of smugglers soon after its founding in the 18th century. Although it later became an important commercial port for incoming slaves and outgoing sugar, the independence of spirit and healthy disregard for authority that the smuggling history had fostered meant the town was always at the forefront of Cuba's rebellions.

The best part of Manzanillo is Parque Céspedes, a lovely, airy square with a marvellous bandstand (the *glorieta*) and several fine buildings in a Moorish style. The Museo Histórico on the square's southeastern side explores the town's history. Near by is the Iglesia de la Purisima Concepción, the town's finest church. About 400m southwest of the square is a memorial to Celia Sánchez, who organised the local underground movement which supported Castro, and was his constant companion after the revolution until her death in 1980.

Southwest of Manzanillo a road runs along the finger of land that juts out into the Caribbean. Here lies La Demajagua, the sugar plantation where Carlos Manual de Céspedes launched the First War of Independence on 10 October 1868. Here a monument is inscribed with a quotation from Fidel Castro: 'We would then have been as they were, they today would be as we are'. You can see the bell that was once rung to summon slaves to work, but was rung by Céspedes to spark the War.

Where To...

Above: *town house in Viñales*

Havana

Prices

Prices are approximate, based on a three-course meal for one without drinks and service:

£   = $10
££   = $10–$20
£££ = over $20

Ice-cream

The Cubans are very fond of ice-cream and every town has a state-run Coppelia ice-cream (*helado*) parlour. There will usually be a queue – the more so at present because economic problems have caused shortages – but the wait and the price will be worth while.

Cafe O'Reilly (£)

Snacks only, no complete meals, but a great stop for a coffee or a drink. Former peso café, refurbished and turned into a dollar café, thus losing many of its Cuban clients. Still very pleasant, however.

✉ **Calle O'Reilly e/ San Ignacio y Cuba, Old Havana** 🕐 11AM–3AM

Don Giovanni (££)

Italian-style menu served in a very pretty late 18th-century Moorish house. A lovely setting with fine views, but the quality of the pastas and pizzas can vary.

✉ **Calle Tacón 4, just off Plaza de la Catedral, Old Havana** ☎ 571036 🕐 12–12

El Aljibe (££)

Thatch-roofed restaurant with excellent Cuban *criollo* food.

✉ **7a 24 y 26 Miramar** ☎ 204 1584 🕐 12PM–12AM

El Floridita (££)

Bar beloved of Hemingway, but it is doubtful whether he would pay today's prices for 'my daiquiri in the Floridita'. Refurbishment has spoiled some of the old charm, but the history is hard to ignore.

✉ **Calle Obispo 557 esq Avenida de Bélgica, Havana Centro** ☎ 867 1300 🕐 12PM–1AM

El Patio (£££)

The most beautiful restaurant in Havana, housed in a fine mid-18th century *palacio*. Unimpressive food, but worth a drink for the ambience.

✉ **Plaza de la Catedral, Old Havana** ☎ 860 6686 🕐 12–12

La Bodeguita del Medio (££)

Overpriced bar – Hemingway would have turned up his nose at the *mojitos* now sold here (or ordered several more, all in the same glass), but it is worth a visit just to feel the atmosphere (➤ 39).

✉ **Calle Empedrado 207, Old Havana** ☎ 867 1374 🕐 10:30AM–1AM

La Casona del 17 (£/££)

In an elegant mansion, the restaurant has a terrace with bar and grill serving cheap (but good) pizzas and chicken, and an indoor restaurant serving a better, more expensive, menu with some traditional Cuban meals – try the *boliche mechado* (beef stuffed with chorizo sausage).

✉ **Calle 17, 60 e/ N y M, Havana-Vedado** ☎ 334529 🕐 9–2AM

La Mina (££)

Cuban food on an elegant garden patio.

✉ **Plaza de Armes** ☎ 620216 🕐 24 hours

Las Ruinas (££)

An old sugar mill has been refurbished in very modern style – a lovely place to eat. The menu is a curious mix of the expensive (lobster) and the cheap (Cuban dishes and pasta/pizza) but everything is well cooked and served.

✉ **Cortina de la Presa, Parque Lenin** ☎ 443026 🕐 11AM–midnight. Closed Mon

La Terraza de Cojímar (££)

Another Hemingway favourite, those on the Trail should try *arroz con bacalao* (salt cod and rice) just as he did. One of a few fish restaurants local to Havana. Great views.

✉ **Calle Real 161, Cojímar** 🕐 Lunch, dinner

WHERE TO EAT & DRINK

Western Cuba

Pinar del Río

La Casona (£)
Opposite the Teatro Milanés. A peso restaurant, in a very nice colonial mansion. Overpriced, but sells good food in Cuban style.

✉ **Calle Martí esq Colón, Pinar del Río** 🕐 12PM–1AM. **Closed Tue**

Rumayor (££)
Claimed by many to have the best cabaret outside Havana, this restaurant (housed in a wooden barn) has an excellent menu with a couple of delicious specialities – *pollo ahumado*, smoked chicken, and *pollo Rumayor*, the house chicken grilled and served with a spicy sauce. Both cabaret and restaurant are open air, adding to the atmosphere.

✉ **About 1km north of Pinar del Río on the road to Viñales** ☎ (082) 63007 🕐 12–10. **Closed Thu**

Varadero

Las Américas (£–£££)
In the library of the Du Pont mansion, the most historic place in town (► 25). Savour the decorations and enjoy the beautiful view. The food (inexpensive snacks at lunch time, extortionately priced dinners in the evening) is good too.

✉ **Avenida Las Américas, Varadero** ☎ (05) 667750 🕐 10AM–11:30PM

El Bodegón Criollo
Said to be connected with La Bodeguita del Medio in Old Havana, but may be playing on the association. Interesting décor, with menu chalked on a blackboard. Specialises in Cuban dishes and does them rather well.

✉ **Avenida de la Playa esq Calle 40, Varadero** ☎ (05) 667784 🕐 12–12

Mi Casita (£)
Very pleasant place right on the beach. Excellent value meat (steak and chicken) and some fish – the local lobster is particularly good. They will also do their best for vegetarians, an unusual gesture.

✉ **Camino del Mar e/ 11 y 12, Varadero** ☎ (05) 613787 🕐 12–10:30

El Retiro Josone (£££)
The most expensive place in town. Beautifully sited in the park and with an excellent international menu. Good, but pricey.

✉ **Parque Josone, Varadero** ☎ (05) 62740 🕐 Lunch, dinner

Viñales

Las Brisas (£)
Good basic food. At the time of writing there was a *paladar* (private family restaurant) next door which offered more imaginative cooking (with a few local specialities) – try it.

✉ **On the main street in Viñales** 🕐 Lunch, dinner

Casa de Don Tomás (£)
In a 19th-century wooden colonial mansion, this is a very friendly place selling fried chicken and other straightforward meals and a few surprises. *Las Delicás de Don Tomás* is a mix of seafood, pork and chicken, sausage of undefined heritage and rice all arranged around fried eggs.

✉ **At the southern end of Viñales** ☎ (08) 936300 🕐 9AM–10PM

Dubious Delicacies
Cuba has several species of snake, none of them dangerous. One – the *majá*, a constrictor – has been known to grow to 4m in length. The island also has a large tree rat, the *jutía*, which can weigh up to 4kg. All over the island, but especially in the Viñales valley, both the rats and snakes are a delicacy. They are now very rare and almost never seen on tourist menus, but it might be as well to ask for a translation of that curious-sounding dish on the menu.

103

Central Cuba

Seafood

Considering Cuba is an island there is an astonishing lack of fish restaurants and fish dishes, although lobster and shrimps feature quite commonly. The problem is that private fishing is illegal – in the past the government thought anybody who owned a boat was likely to sail off to Florida – and state boats catch fish for export. There are several species of turtle in the area and visitors may occasionally see *tortuga* on the menu. Some species are not endangered, but it might be as well not to encourage the catching of any of these delightful creatures.

Cienfuegos
Covadonga (£)

Basic, but very pleasant. Although it serves genuine Cuban cooking, actually best for its paella.

✉ Calle 37 e/ Calle O y Avenida 1a, Cienfuegos (opposite the Hotel Jagua) ☎ (0432) 8238 🕐 Lunch, dinner

Palacio de Valle (££)

In superb surroundings with Moorish and gothic touches. Specialises in seafood (with particular emphasis on lobster). A little on the expensive side.

✉ Calle 37, Cienfuegos (beside the Hotel Jagua) ☎ (0432) 63666 or (432) 3021 🕐 9:45AM–11PM

La Verja (££)

Claimed to be the best place in town, with dozens of dishes. Menu ranges from hamburgers to exotic (and excellent) lobster stew. A variety of vegetables, such as yuca (cassava) and some fresh fruit.

✉ Avenida 54, 3306, Cienfuegos ☎ (0432) 6311 🕐 12–2 and 7–9. Closed Tue

Escambray Mountains
El Río Negro (££)

Romantically sited on the edge of the lake – the restaurant can only be reached by boat from the Hotel Hanabanilla – with wonderful views, a very pleasant atmosphere and some excellent Cuban dishes.

✉ Lake Hanabanilla ☎ (0422) 86932 🕐 Lunch, dinner

Sancti Spíritus
Hanoi (£)

A little way from the interesting parts of the town. Good for a proper meal, though the menu is limited. The best dishes are Cuban.

✉ Calle Isabel Valdiva esq Bartolomé Masó, Sancti Spíritus ☎ (041) 23339 🕐 Lunch, dinner

Merendero el Puente (£)

Specialises in fish and some chicken, basically Cuban.

✉ On a boat under bridge end of Jesus Menendez

Restaurante 1514 (£)

Cuban dishes but often no pork. Strange colonial atmosphere as if time has stood still.

✉ Labori, ☎ (041) 23514

Santa Clara
Colonial 1878 (£)

Pleasant colonial building. Arguably the best food in town with the emphasis on Creole cooking.

✉ Calle Máximo Gómez e/ Independencia y Parque Vidal, Santa Clara ☎ (042) 2428 🕐 Lunch, dinner. Closed Mon

Trinidad
Colonial Trinidad (£)

Shady terrace and beautiful 18th-century colonial building. Good menu, well-prepared food 5 minutes' walk from the main square, opposite the local cigar factory.

✉ Calle Máceo 402 esq Colón, Trinidad ☎ (0419) 2873 🕐 Lunch, dinner

El Jigüe (££)

Lovely little place with a wide-ranging menu from a sandwich or simple meal to an expensive lobster-based dinner.

✉ Plaza El Jigüe (Calle Martínez Villena esq Piro Guinart), Trinidad ☎ (0419) 4315 🕐 11–5

Eastern Cuba

Baracoa
La Punta (£)
The best place in town to eat, though there is no priority for tourists who (unusually) queue with the locals. Always seems to have fresh orange juice and a good Cuban menu. For dessert, try the speciality cucurrucho, made of cocoa, coconut and fresh fruit wrapped in a palm leaf.

✉ In Fuerte de la Punta, the fortress at the northern end of Baracoa ☎ (21) 43335 🕐 12–9

Bayamo
Restaurant 1513 (£)
The best of the three official places to eat in the town. A short distance south of the town centre, but worth the walk. Offers a good, if basic, menu with very respectable Cuban cooking.

✉ Calle General García 176 esq General Lora, Bayamo ☎ (023) 422939 🕐 2–10

Camagüey
Gran Hotel (£)
The hotel has one of the best restaurants (the Salon Caribe) in town and its position (on the 5th floor) adds a superb view to the good food from a reasonable menu.

✉ Calle Máceo 67 e/ Agramonte y Gómez, Camagüey ☎ (0322) 92093 🕐 Lunch, dinner

Holguín
Hotel Pernik (£)
The Sofia Restaurant is the best in town, with a fine Cuban menu and excellent food, usually including a good range of vegetables. The restaurant is huge, but tastefully decorated.

✉ Avenida Jorge Dimitrov esq XX Aniversario, Holguín ☎ (024) 481011

Santiago de Cuba
Don Antonio (£)
Lovely colonial building featuring excellent criollo cooking.

✉ Plaza Dolores ☎ (0226) 652205

El Morro (£)
Next door to the fortress, with the same awe-inspiring view. Cuban cooking with a speciality – Creole-style horsemeat – that may not be to everybody's taste.

✉ Castillo del Morro, to the south of Santiago de Cuba ☎ (0226) 690109 🕐 Lunch, dinner

Hotel Casa Granda (££)
The ground-floor restaurant overlooking Santiago's main square serves excellent food. After your meal, take a drink in the roof garden bar for a marvellous view of the city.

✉ Parque Céspedes, Santiago de Cuba ☎ (0226) 686600 🕐 7–10, 12–3 and 7–11

Restaurant 1900 (£££)
A training centre for chefs, and the best restaurant in Santiago. In a Bacardí family mansion, beautifully furnished, with huge chandeliers. Cuban and international menu. Reservations recommended.

✉ Calle Bartolomé Masó 354 e/ Pío Rosado y Hartmann, Santiago de Cuba ☎ (0226) 623507 🕐 1–3, 6–12. Closed Mon

Tocororo (£££)
To the east of the Hotel Santiago, a little way from the centre. In a delightful colonial mansion, it offers a good menu and well prepared meals.

✉ Avenida Manduley 102, Santiago de Cuba ☎ (0226) 643761 🕐 12–9. Closed Sun

Paladares
One of the most interesting of recent tourist initiatives is the paladar. These are private restaurants with licences to cater for no more than 10 or 12 people (so that Cubans will not employ Cubans, the restaurant being run by family members). Paladares consist of a few tables and chairs in the front room of someone's house. The menu will be basic – chicken and pork, perhaps lobster or shrimp if you are lucky – but the style will be authentic. Some paladares offer food as good as any on the island. But do be cautious: discuss prices beforehand and ask about extras, as some paladar owners are not above fleecing unsuspecting foreigners.

Telephone Codes
The telephone numbers in the book are given with their town dialling codes from Havana. The Havana code from anywhere on the island is 07.

Havana

Prices
Approximate prices per room per night:

£ = $50
££ = $50–$90
£££ = over $90

Camping
Those wanting a back-to-nature holiday should consider camping. Cuba's climate is ideal for it, and there are over a hundred sites spread throughout the country. Many of these have permanent tents that can be hired, and some also have basic bungalows for rent. The sites are used by Cubans for the most part, but if you insist you will almost certainly be allowed to stay.

The following hotels are open throughout the year.

Ambos Mundos (££)
Ernest Hemingway's old haunt in Havana (➤ 38), now completely refurbished (down to the pink façade) with elegant rooms. Wonderful views from the roof terrace.
✉ Calle Obispo 153 esq Mercaderes, Old Havana ☎ 669530

Casa Cientifico (£)
The former academy of sciences with sweeping marble staircase. Second floor budget accommodation (usually for Cubans) with shared bathrooms, cold water only. The third floor has hot water and private bathrooms.
✉ Paseo de Martí 212, Old Havana ☎ 862 4511

Conde de Villanueva (££)
Valencia-style, nine rooms around a courtyard.
✉ Mercaderes 202 e/ Lamparilla y Amargura, Old Havana ☎ 862 9682

Deauville (£)
Its architecture appalled Hemingway's wife, Martha Gellhorn, who reckoned it blighted the Malecón, but this hotel has many admirers.
✉ Avenida de Italia esq Malecón, Havana Centro ☎ 338813

Havana Libre (££)
Vast hotel, central for tourist Havana. Excellent facilities. Home of the revolutionary government immediately after Batista's fall.
✉ Calle L e/ 23 y 25, Havana-Vedado ☎ 333806

Inglaterra (££)
One of the oldest hotels in the capital, and one of the most distinctive buildings. Situated on Parque Central, with a pleasant atmosphere. Excellent piano bar.
✉ Paseo de Martí (Prado) 416 esq Calle San Rafael, Havana-Vedado ☎ 860 8593

Melía Cohiba (£££)
A luxury hotel in a splendid position near the Malecón. Well-appointed, but the North American/European standards come at a price.
✉ Paseo de Martí (Prado) e/ 1 y 3, Havana-Vedado ☎ 333636

Morro (£)
Surprisingly cheap considering the service, because of its position off the tourist track, still close to the Malecón.
✉ Calle 3 esq D, Havana-Vedado ☎ 333907

Nacional (£££)
Where Winston Churchill and Frank Sinatra stayed, one of the landmarks of Havana. Every conceivable facility, but prices to match.
✉ Calle O esq 21, Havana-Vedado ☎ 873 3564

Santa Isabel (£££)
Housed in the *palacio* of Count Santovenia, one of the most prestigious hotels in Havana. Close to all the main sights, and with good restaurant, café, and a bar.
✉ Plaza de Armas, Old Havana ☎ 338201

Valencia (£)
Small hotel in an 18th-century colonial mansion. A very good restaurant specialising in paella. Book early as the few rooms are very popular.
✉ Calle Oficios 53 e/ Lamparilla y Obrapía, Old Havana ☎ 867 1037

Western Cuba

Bahia de Cochinos
Villa Playa Girón (£)
Fairly basic, with rooms in concrete bungalows, but ideal for the simple life. The restaurant is adequate, but the bar is very good.

✉ **Playa Girón** ☎ **(059) 4110**

Cayo Largo
Villa Capricho
Visitors stay in Amerindian-style thatched cabins on the beach, each with a hammock swinging from the cabin A-frame. There is an excellent restaurant, guests can use the water sports facilities of the Hotel Isla del Sur.

✉ **Cayo Largo** ☎ **794215**

Guamá
Villa Guamá (£)
The ideal place from which to explore the beautiful Zapata Peninsula, but also close to the idyllic Bay of Pigs beaches. Swimming pool and boating on the lake. Guests stay in Amerindian-style thatched cabins.

✉ **At Treasure Lake, north of the Bay of Pigs** ☎ **(059) 2979**

Pinar del Río
Hotel el Mirador (£)
Canopied hotel on a hill by the town's mineral springs and spa (range of health and beauty treatments). Good restaurant, excellent pizzas.

✉ **San Diego de los Baños**
☎ **33 5410**

Sierra del Rosario
Moka Ecolodge (££)
A remarkable development within the UNESCO biosphere reserve, reached by winding paths through the vegetation. A small hotel which will suit nature lovers and those who want to get away from it all. Excellent Creole restaurant.

Air-conditioned rooms with full facilities.

✉ **Near Las Terrazas, Sierra del Rosario** ☎ **(082) 852996**

Varadero
Bella Costa (£££)
Large, modern resort complex with landscaped gardens, swimming pool and beach. Very well appointed rooms and excellent restaurant.

✉ **Avenida Las Américas, Varadero** ☎ **(05) 667210**

SuperClubs Club Varadero (£££)
The ultimate in luxury and sophistication. SuperClubs run all-inclusive resorts – no extras, not even tips – and offer a full range of sports equipment for free hire.

✉ **Carretera Las Américas 3km, Varadero** ☎ **(053) 566 7030**

Villa Cuba (££)
Rooms in large villas which have communal areas. Ideal for groups or those who like shared accommodation.

✉ **Avenida 1 esq Calle C, Varadero** ☎ **(05) 668280**

Viñales
La Ermita (£)
On a hilltop with superb valley views. Fully air-conditioned rooms, excellent restaurant (Cuban and international menus) and swimming pool.

✉ **About 2km east of Viñales**
☎ **(082) 936071**

Los Jazmines (£)
Stunning views of the Viñales Valley. Explore the countryside (hire horses from the hotel), relax by the pool, or enjoy a meal in the restaurant. Air-conditioned.

✉ **About 4km south of Viñales**
☎ **(082) 936210**

Addresses
Cuban addresses have been known to drive visitors to distraction, but they are really quite straightforward. The first named street is the one into which the building faces. The number might be given, but not always. If the building is on the corner of another street the name of this is given after esq (meaning corner). Otherwise, the streets to the left and right are given, so that you can work out on which block of the town's grid the building stands. Thus *e/ Calle 1 y Calle 3* means between streets 1 and 3. This is usually shortened to *e/ 1 y 3*.

Central Cuba

Women's Lib
Wives who prefer hotels to self-catering holidays, because they offer a change from doing all the housework, might be interested to know that in Cuba there is a law requiring husbands to help with the household chores.

Cienfuegos
Jagua (££)
Arguably the best hotel in central Cuba (built by Batista's brother in the 1950s) and well sited on the peninsula at the southern end of town, next to the Palacio de Valle.
✉ **Calle 37, 1, Cienfuegos** ☎ **(0432) 545 1003**

Rancho Luna (£)
Situated just a few steps from the area's best beach. Diving equipment can be hired and there are other sports facilities available. The rooms are air-conditioned and there is a restaurant and nightclub.
✉ **Playa Rancho Luna, near Cienfuegos** ☎ **(0432) 545 1212**

Escambray Mountains
Hanabanilla (£)
Transport is essential unless you are interested only in fishing, walking, horse riding and the occasional boat trip. Beautifully sited, though the Soviet-style architecture is not aesthetically pleasing. The views from the rooftop bar are superb.
✉ **Lake Hanabanilla in the Escambray Mountains** ☎ **(0422) 86932**

Los Helechos (£)
In the health spa of Topes, with a thermal swimming pool, steam baths and gym. The cooler air will be welcomed by those wanting an active holiday in the Escambray Mountains and by those simply wanting a quiet respite from the sun and sand on the coast.
✉ **Topes de Collantes** ☎ **(0419) 40330**

Morón
Morón (£)
Modern hotel at the southern edge of the town and well sited for exploration of the north coast.
✉ **Avenida de Tarafa, Morón** ☎ **(033) 3901**

Remedios
Mascotte (£)
The only hotel in town, but situated in the main square and occupying a beautifully restored, 19th-century building. Very atmospheric.
✉ **Parque Martí, Remedios** ☎ **(042) 395481**

Sancti Spíritus
Motel Los Laureles (£)
Shaded by trees from the noon sun and with a good swimming pool. Your own transport is recommended.
✉ **About 5km north of Sancti Spíritus** ☎ **(041) 395144/395467**

Santa Clara
Santa Clara Libre (£)
Stay in a part of history: the façade maintains the bullet holes from Guevara's battle for the town! Excellent restaurant and stunning views from the rooftop bar, but stay as high up as possible to avoid the basement disco.
✉ **Parque Vidal 6 e/ Marta Abreu y Tristá, Santa Clara** ☎ **(0422) 27548**

Trinidad
Motel Las Cuevas (£)
Situated on a hill top with an incomparable view of the town and the Caribbean. Air-conditioned rooms either in cabins or apartment style. Very popular with independent travellers.
✉ **About 1km northeast of Trinidad, beyond the Iglesia de Santa Ana** ☎ **(0419) 4013**

Eastern Cuba

Baracoa
El Castillo (£)
Irresistible hotel in a clifftop 18th-century fort with wonderful views of the town and El Yunque. The clifftop position adds a little air to the hottest of days and is very pleasant in the evenings.

✉ **Calle Calixto García, Baracoa** ☎ **(021) 42147 or 42103**

Bayamo
Sierra Maestra (£)
Well situated to explore the revolutionary sites. Fairly basic but friendly and comfortable hotel with a swimming pool.

✉ **About 3km east of Bayamo** ☎ **(023) 423102**

Camagüey
Gran Hotel (£)
Not as grand as the name, but very comfortable. Within easy reach of the centre of town and with a good 5th-floor restaurant that offers a superb view.

✉ **Calle Máceo 67 e/ Agramonte y Gómez, Camagüey** ☎ **(0322) 337718**

Holguín
Delta Las Brisas (£££)
A new all-inclusive resort hotel on a beautiful stretch of beach. Excellent facilities including watersports equipment hire, tennis and horse riding: especially good for families with children. Several good restaurants and a nightly disco.

✉ **Guardalavaca** ☎ **(024) 30218**

Sol Río de Mares/Sol Club Río de Luna (££)
Architecturally interesting twin resorts built around large swimming pools just a few steps from the beach. Sports and diving facilities and diving tuition (at the de Mares) to certificate standard. The de Luna specialises in activities for children.

✉ **Playa Estero Ciego, about 6km southwest of Guardalavaca** ☎ **(024) 30062**

Playa Sevilla
Sierra Mar (£££)
SuperClubs all inclusive resort, magically sited on a hillside terrace with its own beach. Numerous sports facilities and free loan of watersports equipment. The ultimate in luxury. There is a second SuperClubs resort near by – Los Galeones (☎ (022) 26160) – which is much smaller and perched on a rocky bluff. The facilities of Sierra Mar are available to guests at Los Galeones.

✉ **Playa Sevilla, about 70km southwest of Santiago de Cuba** ☎ **(022) 29110**

Santiago de Cuba
Hotel Casa Granda (££)
Elegant hotel overlooking Santiago's main square. The elegance extends to the rooms and furnishings, making it one of the best places to stay while exploring the city.

✉ **Parque Céspedes, Santiago de Cuba** ☎ **(0226) 686600**

Santiago de Cuba (£££)
The most luxurious hotel in town, but a little away from the centre. The view from the Pico Real bar on the 15th floor is superb. Well-appointed rooms and good buffet-style meals.

✉ **Avenida de Las Américas esq Calle M, Santiago de Cuba** ☎ **(0226) 687070**

Street Names
After the 1959 revolution many of the street names in Cuban towns were changed, pride of place in the new naming being given to heroes of the Wars of Independence. Now every town has its Parque Martí and Parque Céspedes. Many of these names have been adopted by the locals, but a few of the older names were so ingrained that there has been a reluctance to use the new ones. The prime example is the Paseo de Martí in Havana-Vedado, which is still almost universally known as the Prado. In this book the local, common name is used, or both names are given where confusion is possible.

A Communist Economy

Exotic Gifts

Of the more curious and exotic items that can be bought, be particularly wary of crocodile-skin articles, or any coral. Crocodile-skin gifts from the official crocodile farms, for example at Treasure Lake (► 61), are acceptable, but make sure you obtain a certificate from the shop. Many corals, particularly black coral, are endangered, though they continue to be sold. The best policy is not to buy coral, but if you do you must get a certificate or you may be stopped at customs. Bear in mind, too, that you may have difficulty importing your gift at home.

One of the by-products of the state-run economy is an absence of consumerism and private enterprise. The result is a lack of goods (and a lack of choice) in most Cuban shops. Visitors are also not encouraged to trade in pesos (and the official rate makes purchases far too expensive), so most things you buy will come from dollar shops, found at almost all hotels – certainly all the resort hotels – and in the major towns. There's no mistaking a dollar shop: its bright exterior and air-conditioning contrast completely with other shops.

Souvenirs

The best buys are T-shirts with portraits of Che – usually the famous Korda picture – or political slogans, and the revolutionary posters. If you want something more specifically Cuban you will need to find a craft outlet. That in Havana's Plaza Vieja (**Fondo Cubano de Bienes Culturales**) is very good for arts and crafts, as is **Gallería La Acacia** at San Martín 114, behind the Gran Teatro. In Santiago de Cuba, **Artesanía Santiago** in Calle Felix Peña, near the cathedral, and the **Communidad Artística Verraco** in Parque Baconao sell good local art and craftwork. In Trinidad the **Taller Alfarero** sells a range of pottery, crafted and fired at the site. Much is of the souvenir type with 'Cuba' or 'Trinidad' written on it, but there is also the odd gem. Cayo Largo has Cuba's only shop selling objects associated with the Santería cult. The market at **Tacon** is a good place to buy arts and crafts, especially tiny comic figurines of Fidel and Che. Obtain a receipt for all works of art: you may be stopped at customs on your way home and have the article confiscated without compensation if you cannot authenticate it.

Coffee, Cigars & Rum

Cuban coffee is rarely available in Europe or North America, but it is excellent and very good value.

Cigar buyers should be cautious. Street vendors will offer 'genuine' cigars at fractions of the factory and dollar shop prices, but these are fakes. Genuine cigars come with a special receipt which means that fakes are always detected and confiscated by Cuban customs at the airport. The cigars on sale are the familiar brands but at much lower prices than in Europe or North America. Lesser known varieties, such as Vegueros from the factory in Pinar del Río, are also worth considering.

Rum comes in three ages: 3-, 5- and 7-year. Distilled from cane sugar, rum is colourless, the colour of the older versions coming from added colourants. Havana Club is the best-known label, but Ron Varadero is also very good.

The tourist literature claims that rum and cigar prices are the same in the dollar shops as in duty free shops, since the dollar shops' prices are free of duty. This is usually true for those departing from Varadero, but not for Havana airport, where the prices are slightly lower, but there is a smaller range.

Children's Attractions

In many ways Cuba is the ideal destination for visitors with children: the days are sunny, the beaches clean, the sea warm and (usually) safe. The Cubans love children (the more so if they are small and blonde) and are very protective of them. The downside is that the developing tourist industry has concentrated on the building of hotels wih the aim of maximising hard currency income, rather than providing facilities specifically for holidaymakers. As a consequence, there are not, as yet, the custom-built theme parks, water parks and so on that parents usually find useful for keeping children entertained. Such few places as do exist are listed below.

Adventure Trips

All the larger resort hotels offer equipment for water sports, and most also offer tuition in windsurfing, water-skiing, jet-skiing, snorkelling and diving. Visitors to Varadero can take a day trip to the Bellamar Caves, while those to Havana could have a longer day to the west, taking in the Cueva del Indio in the Viñales Valley. Older and more adventurous children might also enjoy a real caving expedition. Ask at the Havanatur/Infotur office near your resort (or at the hotel itself) for details on trips in your area. Alternatively, rafting (including white water rafting) is available on several of Cuba's rivers.

Varasub

This will be an adventure for most children. The Varasub is a surface boat with underwater seats and portholes allowing passengers a close-up view of the sea life near the reefs of Varadero. Reservations can be made at most hotels in Varadero and Havana, or from the Tour and Travel stands in Varadero and Havana, or through Havanatur.

⊠ **Hotel Paradiso, Varadero**
🕐 **Six trips daily, each lasting 1½ hours.**

Aquaria

To the east of Santiago de Cuba, at the eastern side of Parque Baconao, the Acuario Baconao has regular shows with dolphins and sea lions. There is also an aquarium with fish and lobsters, and a tank of sharks. The highlight of the visit is the chance to swim with the dolphins for a remarkably small fee. Near Havana, the Acuario Nacional has regular dolphin shows as well as the more usual tanks.

Acuario Baconao
⊠ **Parque Baconao**
🕐 **Tue–Sun 9–4. There are dolphin shows at 10:15, 11:30 and 2:45.**

Acuario Nacional
⊠ **Avenida 1 esq Calle 60, Havana-Miramar** ☎ **230 6401**
🕐 **Tue–Sun 10–6** 🚌 **9 or 420**

Fun Park

To the east of Santiago, El Mundo de la Fantasia is a Disney-style fun park with the usual rides; there is also a small zoo and amusement park.

El Mundo de la Fantasia
⊠ **Parque Baconao** 🕐 **Daily 10–5**

Toilets

There are few public toilets in Cuba, and those that do exist do not approach the standard usually found in Europe or North America. It is generally best to ask at the nearesr hotel or restaurant. Always carry toilet paper as it is rarely supplied, as well as hand-cleaning wipes in case the water supply is not functioning. Do not put toilet paper down the lavatory or you will block it – always use the small wastebin at the side.

Sport

Information

Cartelera, a free newspaper containing listings of films showing at local cinemas, theatre shows, museum and gallery exhibitions and night clubs, as well as restaurants and hotels, can be obtained free in Havana. Try the reception desk of your hotel, or any hotel you happen to pass.

Caving

There is a large number of caves, some very beautiful, underneath Cuba. Some, such as the Cuevas de Bellamar near Varadero, are open to the public, but many are not and can only be entered with experienced leaders. For such expeditions no experience is necessary and all equipment is supplied. Ask at your hotel for details of available trips.

Cycling

The lack of traffic makes Cuba ideal for cycling. Most resort hotels will hire out bicycles, or you might be able to buy one in Havana or other large town and sell it back at the end of the holiday. From the hotels in Varadero, bicycles are the best way of exploring the eastern end of the peninsula: take a packed lunch and a towel and find your own section of unspoilt beach.

Diving

Cuba is ideal for diving, its warm, clear waters adding to the delights of coral reefs and ancient wrecks. Most top-of-the-range resort hotels offer diving tuition or organised dives. The following centres will be able to help both experienced and novice divers.

Centro Internacional Buceo
✉ Maria La Gorda ☎ (082) 5771

Centro Internacional Buceo
✉ Playa Esterio Ciego, Guardalavaca ☎ (024) 30102

Centro de Buceo
✉ Playa Girón ☎ (059) 2979

Centro de Buceo Delphis
✉ Calle 24 esq Camino del Mar, Varadero ☎ (05) 63481 or 337072

Centro de Buceo Punta Frances
✉ Hotel El Colony, Island of Youth ☎ (061) 398181/2

Centro Internacional Buceo Los Galeones
✉ Parque Baconao, Santiago de Cuba ☎ (0226) 335209

Delphis Diving Centre
✉ Guardalavaca ☎ (024) 30114 or 30130

Hotel Isla del Sur
✉ Cayo Largo ☎ 333156

Marlin Dive Centre
✉ Hemingway Marina, Havana-Miramar ☎ 225090

Villa Guajimico
Scuba-oriented resort, with 150 bungalows in gardens by the sea.
✉ Cumanayagua Cienfuegos ☎ (0432) 451002; fax (0432 451206)

There are decompression chambers at the Hotel El Colony on the Island of Youth and at the Naval Hospital in Havana. Those who wish to enjoy the sea life of the Varadero reefs without the need for diving or snorkelling should try the Varasub (▶ 111).

Fishing

For the best freshwater fishing, head for Lago Hanabanilla (☎ 86932 for details), Presa Zaza near Sancti Spíritus, for the lakes near Morón (☎ 28013 for details) or Guamá (Treasure Lake). For $65 per day you can fish from a boat in Rio Tijuanico in Guamá. The main fish in these waters is the largemouth bass, known as *trucha* to the Cubans.

Those wanting to try their hand against something larger should consider deep sea fishing for marlin or swordfish. Such trips will last all day and visitors should be well prepared. Take plenty of refreshment, or ensure that the boat has a well-stocked fridge, take a hat, and be prepared for a struggle: big fish can take hours to land. There are several centres on the island where boats can be hired, including Marina Hemingway in Havana-Miramar, Marinas Gaviota and Acua in Varadero, Playa del Este near Havana, the Island of Youth and Cayo Largo.

Horse Riding

Many hotels, particularly the resort hotels, have horses for hire. Riding is an excellent way of exploring the Cuban countryside and the stables take riders from beginners to expert.

Sky Diving

The ultimate thrill – see Cuba from 3,000m up while dropping headlong towards it. Sky diving is now on offer from Varadero's old airport, novice parachutists being strapped to an expert. The experience is not cheap (though you do get a free T-shirt and a certificate). For details contact:

Centro Internacional de Paracaidismo
✉ **The old airport to the west of Varadero** ☎ **(05) 667256/ 667260/664282**

Walking

Cuba is a walker's paradise, with its lush vegetation, relatively low mountains, and exotic birds and butterflies, However, the limited number of trails and lack of adequate maps mean that the truly wild areas are for the experienced only. A difficult but spectacular 3-day trek is possible through the Sierra Maestra, including Pico Turquino, Cuba's highest peak. Government guides are required, and reservations must be made in advance through Centro de Inspección y Control Ambiental in Havana (☎ 204 2676). Keen hikers should not be put off by the present lack of infrastructure. Provided you take care, trips can be very rewarding – but take insect repellent.

Water Sports

Cuba's lack of private enterprise means that there are no watersports schools or hiring companies. However, most resort hotels have their own facilities where equipment can be borrowed and tuition is available.

Cuba's Atlantic coast offers excellent **surfing** from December to March, when the northeast trade winds pile water on to the shore.

The north coast resorts – Varadero and Guardalavaca – and those on the south – Cayo Largo and Santiago – offer excellent **windsurfing**, especially between December and March, when wind and weather are reliable.

Yachts can be chartered at Varadero and Cayo Largo, but they are expensive (though most can take 6–10 people). The experience of sweeping across the Caribbean or Atlantic is unforgettable.

Sea Safety

Most Cuban beaches have a flag system to warn of water conditions. Green and red mean that swimming is safe or unsafe respectively. An orange flag means that conditions are changing, or that care should be taken. Most beaches also have lifeguards: if you are unsure, ask their advice and be sure to take it.

Nightlife

Musical Memories
The Cubans are always willing to pass on their musical traditions to visitors and offer courses in everything from drumming to traditional wind instruments. These courses are cheap, a good way of making friends, and leave you with a lasting souvenir of your trip.

Cabaret
It could be argued that there is only one cabaret in Cuba – the Tropicana in Havana – all the others being mere imitations. The style of the show is certainly very similar in all the cabarets, but it is always worth trying something new. Below are listed the best of the island's cabarets.

Havana
Cabaret Nacional (Parisien)
✉ Calle San Rafael esq Prado, Old Havana (near the Gran Teatro, opposite the Hotel Inglaterra) ☎ 333564

Papa's
✉ Marina Hemingway, Havana-Miramar ☎ 225591

Tropicana
✉ Calle 72, 4504, Havana-Vedado ☎ 267 1717

Pinar del Río
Rumayor
✉ On the road towards Viñales ☎ (82) 63007

Santiago de Cuba
Club 300
✉ Aguillera 302 ☎ (0226) 653532

Tropicana
✉ On the Autopista Nacional, 2km from the centre of Santiago ☎ (0226) 686573

Trinidad
La Cueva
✉ Hotel Las Cuevas, Trinidad ☎ (0419) 2340 or 3624

Varadero
Cabaret Varadero
✉ Via Blanca y Carreteria Cárdenas, Varadero (in the Anfiteatro, near the river bridge) ☎ (05) 62169

Continental
✉ Hotel International, Avenida Los Américas, Varadero ☎ (05) 667039

Cueva del Pirata
✉ On the Autopista Sur at the 11km point (just east of the Hotel Sol Palmerias), Varadero ☎ (06) 667751

Viñales
Cueva San Miguel (Cueva de Viñales)
✉ Viñales ☎ (082) 93203

Dance
The world-famous Cuban National Ballet performs at the Gran Teatro in Havana, but also visits other large towns, while the Ballet Folklórico Cutumba, specialising in ballet based upon more traditional Cuban dance patterns, has its home in Santiago de Cuba.

Clave y Guaguanco
National folkloric dance troupe who perform in Havana on Sundays.
✉ Callzjón de Hammel, Aramburo y Hospital, Centro Habana ⏰ Sun 11AM

The most distinctive of the traditional dances is the rumba, which is likely to be included in any cabaret show. The audience at a cabaret may also be invited to join a conga starting on stage and snaking among the seats.

Discos
The line between a disco and a cabaret can be blurred, but some of the most authentic discos are listed below.

Havana
Havana Club
✉ Hotel Comodoro, Calle 84

esq 1a, Havana-Miramar
☎ 225551

Palacio de la Salsa
✉ Hotel Riviera, Avenida Paseo esq Malecón, Havana-Vedado ☎ 334051

Santiago de Cuba
Club El Iris
✉ Aguilera 617, near Plaza de Marte ☎ (0226) 53500

Varadero
Havana Club
✉ Centro Comercial Copey, Avenida 3 esq Calle 62, Varadero ☎ (05) 667009

La Bamba
✉ Hotel Tuxpan, Varadero
☎ (05) 667560

Viñales
Cueva San Miguel (Cueva de Viñales)
✉ Viñales ☎ (082) 93203

Music
Cuba was the birthplace of several types of music, which have gone on to achieve world recognition. Rumba, invented by black workers in sugar mills in the 19th century, is strongly based on Congo drum-based rhythms.

The Spanish settlers on Cuba took with them the folk song traditions of Spain, specifically the *trova*, a romantic form of ballad associated with the troubadours of medieval Europe. The fusion of trova and the more upbeat rhythms of Afro-Cuba gave rise to son, a name hardly recognised outside the island even though *The Peanut Vendor* is widely known. Son eventually fathered mambo, cha-cha-cha and, more recently, salsa (meaning sauce, a reference to its being hot and spicy).

Cuban jazz has also been influential, a form known as Latin Jazz influenced Dizzy Gillespie, one of the pioneers of bebop.

Some of these beats will be heard in cabarets and nightclubs, but can also be heard – usually in more authentic forms, together with other, more 'folk'-based music (trova) – in the Casa de la Trova or Casa de la Cultura that can be found in every town on the island.

Nightclubs
Below are listed the best places to hear live music, ranging from authentic Cuban to jazz, while enjoying something to eat and, perhaps, a dance.

Havana
Havana Café
✉ Hotel Meliá Cohiba
☎ 333636

Piano Bar Neptuno
✉ Hotel Neptuno, Calle 3 esq 70, Havana-Miramar ☎ 247726

Santiago de Cuba
Cafe Cantante
✉ Avenida Américas esq Desfiles, Santiago de Cuba
☎ (0226) 644 3178

Pico Real
✉ Hotel Santiago, Santiago de Cuba ☎ (0226) 642656 or 642612

Varadero
Hemi
✉ Calle C e/ Avenida 62 y 63, Varadero ☎ (05) 63012

Vertigo
✉ Hotel Bellamar, Calle 17 e/ 1a y 3a, Varadero ☎ (05) 667490

Theatres
Cuba has over 50 theatres, a rise of several hundred per cent over the number pre-revolution. Every large town has at least one. Attractions range from amateur productions of Spanish plays to full-scale operas. Hotels (or the theatre billboard) will supply details.

Getting Around
Cuban buses were notoriously unreliable, but have greatly improved since the import of buses from Holland, Spain and Sweden (still with original ads inside and destinations on the front). Queues only occur now at peak times. For a real adventure try the unique Cuban metrobus, which resembles an inverted camel. Where time is important, taxis are the best way to travel, but if you can afford to be a bit more relaxed, take a *coche*, a horse-drawn taxi. The *cochero* (driver) will usually restrict his use of the whip on the horse if you say you are in no hurry and offer a tip. In Havana, the *coche* has recently been joined by the rickshaw cycle, a twin passenger vehicle with a single pedalling 'driver'.

What's On When

Carnival Revived
As part of the austerity programme of the Special Period (announced in 1991) Cuban carnivals were banned. The ban has now been lifted (chiefly, it is said, because carnivals are popular with tourists) and although economic problems have lessened the number of costumes, bands and fireworks, it has not dampened the general enthusiasm.

January
At New Year, Cubans have a traditional meal formerly held at Christmas. It is also the anniversary of the revolution. Cultural events celebrate the birthday of José Martí (28 Jan). The Varadero Carnival starts in late January with events continuing into February.

February
The Jornados de la Cultura Camagüetana: A fortnight of cultural events in Camagüey. Carnival in Havana.
Festival Internacional de Jazz Plaza: biennially, Havana. Celebrations of the Second War of Independence (24 Feb).

March
Events to celebrate the attack on the Presidential Palace in 1957 (13 Mar).

April
Celebration of the Bay of Pigs victory (19 Apr).

May
May Day Parade – a carnival mixture of Marxism and salsa. The parade assembles from 6AM, the march lasts from 9AM to about midday. Anyone can join and parade past the dignitaries (including Fidel Castro) in the Plaza de la Revolución. Pilgrimage of *Romería de Mayo* to Loma de la Cruz, Holguín (3 May). Bands and orchestras play in the town squares. The Ernest Hemingway International Marlin Fishing Tournament in Havana-Miramar.

June
Fiestas Sanjuaneras in Trinidad, the town's Carnival.

July
Revived carnival in Santiago de Cuba (still a shadow of its old self, but improving). Also a Festival of Caribbean Culture. Events to celebrate Martyrs of the Revolution Day (26 Jul). Holiday from 26–28 Jul.

August
Festival Internacional Musica Popular Benny Moré in Cienfuegos. Benny Moré, who died in 1963, was the leading exponent of mambo. Bands from around the world, but especially Latin America.

September
Festival Internacional Teatro: A biennial festival of theatre in Havana (late Aug–early Sep).

October
Events to remember the death of Che Guevara (8 Oct). Anniversary of the First War of Independence (10 Oct, national holiday)
Children throw flowers into the sea in memory of Camilo Cienfuegos, who died in a plane crash in 1959. (28 Oct). October sees cultural events in many towns, including a ballet festival and a festival of modern music in Havana, a Spanish-American Festival in Holguín, a theatre and popular music festival in Matanzas.

November
Semana de la Cultura (last two weeks): Cuba's artistic heritage is celebrated in Trinidad.
Festival de Musica Caribe: A festival of Caribbean music held in Varadero.

December
Festival Internacional de Cinematográfica: in Havana.
Festival Internacional de Corros (International Choir Festival): in Santiago de Cuba.
Parrandas in Remedios (►77). Christmas Day (since 1997).

Practical Matters

Above: *typical house in Calle Obispo, Havana*
Right: *a Trinidad potter at work*

117

TIME DIFFERENCES

GMT	Cuba	Germany	USA (NY)	Netherlands	Spain
12 noon	← 7AM	→ 1PM	← 7AM	→ 1PM	→ 1PM

BEFORE YOU GO

WHAT YOU NEED

	UK	Germany	Canada	Netherlands	Spain
● Required, ○ Suggested, ▲ Not required — Some countries require a passport to remain valid for a minimum period (usually at least six months) beyond the date of entry – contact their consulate or embassy or your travel agent for details.					
Passport valid for 3 months beyond period of stay	●	●	●	●	●
Tourist Card (for holiday travel up to 4 weeks)	●	●	●	●	●
Tourist Visa (for visits longer than 3 weeks or for stay with Cuban family)	●	●	●	●	●
Onward or Return Ticket	●	●	●	●	●
Health Inoculations	▲	▲	▲	▲	▲
Health Documentation	▲	▲	▲	▲	▲
Travel Insurance	○	○	○	○	○
Driving Licence (national, but international recommended)	●	●	●	●	●
Car Insurance Certificate (with car rental)	○	○	○	○	○

WHEN TO GO

Havana

■ High season
☐ Low season

JAN	FEB	MAR	APR	MAY	JUN	JUL	AUG	SEP	OCT	NOV	DEC
26°C	26°C	27°C	29°C	30°C	31°C	32°C	32°C	31°C	29°C	28°C	26°C

 Cloud   Sun   Sunshine & showers

TOURIST OFFICES

In the UK
Cuban Tourist Board
154 Shaftesbury Avenue
London WC2H 8JT
☎ 020 7240 6655
Fax: 020 7836 9265
e-mail:
tourism@cubasi.info

In Canada
Cuban Tourist Board
55 Queens Street East,
No 705, Toronto
Ontario M5H 1R6
☎ 0416 362 0700
Fax: 0416 362 6799
e-mail: info@gocuba.ca

POLICE 116

FIRE 115

AMBULANCE 118

WHEN YOU ARE THERE

ARRIVING

Most visitors arrive by air. There are two international airports – Havana and Varadero, the latter catering mainly for package tour flights.

José Martí Airport, Havana	**Journey times**
Kilometres to city centre	
25 kilometres	🚇 N/A
	🚌 1 hour
	🚗 45 minutes

Juan Gualberto Gómez Airport, Varadero	**Journey times**
Kilometres to resort centre	🚇 N/A
12 kilometres	🚌 30 minutes
	🚗 20 minutes

MONEY

There are three currencies in Cuba. Cubans use the peso (worth 100 centavos), which has an official exchange rate of 1:1 with the US dollar. There are now official Bureaux de Exchange called Cadeca found everywhere, which change dollars to pesos at around 20:1 and pesos to dollars at 25:1. Black market rates are usually lower by a peso because of long queues at Cadecas. Convertible pesos, issued in change dollar shops, have an actual exchange rate of 1:1, so can be used in shops just as US dollars. Convertible pesos can only be converted in Cuba and will be useless if you take them home. US dollars are accepted in all dollar shops, hotels and restaurants. Pesos can be used to buy street food and goods in farmers' markets.

Credit cards are generally only accepted at tourist sites; cards or travellers' cheques issued by American Express or any other US bank will not be accepted.

TIME

Cuban local time is the same as Eastern Standard Time in the US, which is 5 hours behind Greenwich Mean Time (GMT–5). Clocks are turned forward an hour in late March/early April and back an hour in early October.

CUSTOMS

 YES

There are specific allowances of alcohol, tobacco and luxury goods into the country for visitors over the age of 18:

Alcohol: 3L
Cigarettes: 200 *or*
Cigars: 50 *or*
Tobacco: 250 grams
Perfume: unspecified
Gifts totalling not more than $100 together with up to 10kg of medicine (excluding blood-based products)

 NO

A long and varied list, which includes drugs (other than personal medicines) firearms and ammunition, plants or animals (whether alive or dead) and unprocessed food.

EMBASSIES

UK	☎ 332410 or 331771
Germany	☎ 332569 or 332539
Canada	☎ 332516 or 332527
Netherlands	☎ 332511
Spain	☎ 338029

WHEN YOU ARE THERE

TOURIST OFFICES

Since most tourism to Cuba is packaged, there are few tourist offices, the main resort and town hotels providing a local service. However, as most tours are run by Havanatur/Infotur, their offices are a good place to try if you are in need of further information.
Try the following branches:

Havana
Calle Obispo 358
(e/ Habana y Compostella)
Old Havana
☎ 333 3333

Calle 252 esq Cuba
Old Havana
☎ 611544

Calle Galiano esq
San Rafael
Havana Centro
☎ 633095

Calle 23 esq P
Havana-Vedado
☎ 554010

Varadero
Calle 23 esq Avenida
Primera (1er)

Santiago de Cuba
Plaza de Martí
☎ 23302

NATIONAL HOLIDAYS

J	F	M	A	M	J	J	A	S	O	N	D
1				1		1			1		

Cuba's official National Holidays are:

1 Jan	New Year's Day
1 May	International Labour Day
26 Jul	Assault on the Moncada Barracks
10 Oct	Start of First War of Independence
25 Dec	Christmas Day

In addition, there are 'unofficial' holidays on 31 December, 25 July and 27 July. There are also a large number of other significant days (such as the birthday of José Martí on 28 January, Bay of Pigs Victory on 19 April, and so on) when some or all official shops and offices will close.

OPENING HOURS

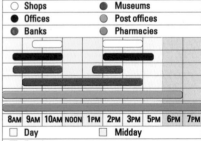

○ Shops	● Museums
● Offices	○ Post offices
● Banks	○ Pharmacies

| 8AM | 9AM | 10AM | NOON | 1PM | 2PM | 3PM | 5PM | 6PM | 7PM |

☐ Day ☐ Midday
☐ Evening

Shop opening times are flexible, depending on whether the shop has anything to sell, but dollar shops catering for tourists generally stay open longer. Banks in resorts also tend to stay open longer than 3PM. Both shops and offices usually close every other Saturday. Post offices in some large towns stay open until 10PM. Pharmacies provide a 24-hour service on a rota basis.
Museum opening times tend to be erratic, particularly for the smaller ones, which may open whenever the curator feels like it.

DRIVE ON THE
RIGHT

NO STARS

TOILETS
FREE

PUBLIC TRANSPORT

Internal Flights Cubana fly between all the major towns of Cuba; their fleet of ex-Soviet aircraft is gradually being updated to more modern Fokker F27s. Fares are relatively cheap, considering the distances involved, and the timetables are generally reliable. Cubana's main office is at the bottom of La Rampa (Calle 23) in Havana-Vedado at No 64 e/ P y Infanta.

Trains Cuba is the only Caribbean island with a railway system. All major towns are linked to Havana by reasonably efficient services. The trains are cheap and comfortable, if slow, and have some delightful touches, such as the man who brings around a flask of coffee but has no cups – supply your own or go thirsty. Checking in 1 hour before departure is vital.

Buses Horror stories of unreliable, overcrowded Cuban buses are no longer true. There is a system of town and long-haul buses, even linking Havana with Santiago. Long-distance buses are still slow but those with dollars can ensure a seat. Be sure to check in an hour before departure.

Ferries Hydrofoils run twice daily from the southern port of Surgidero de Batabanó to the Isla de la Juventud (Island of Youth). The hydrofoils leave at 10AM and 4PM, and the trip takes about 2 hours, the return trips being at 1PM and 7PM. Ferries also run frequently across Havana Bay, from Old Havana to Casablanca and Regla, for only 50 Cuban centavos each way.

CAR RENTAL

Havanautos are the best of the limited number of car rental companies, offering a range of vehicles from the cheap Daewoo Tico to large Mercedes and Dodge Caravans. Four-wheel drive Daihatsus are also available for those contemplating dirt roads. You can rent from one town and drop off at another, but at a price.

TAXIS

Official taxis are readily available at hotels. The best and cheapest are Panataxi (☎ 555555). There are also unofficial taxis plying for hire (usually away from the hotels as they are not allowed near them).The price should be fixed in advance, and they will not take you to beaches or airports, which are heavily policed.

DRIVING

Speed limit on *autopista*: **100kph**
Speed limit on paved roads: **90kph**

Speed limit on dirt roads: **60kph**

Speed limits on urban roads: **50kph** (but **40kph** near schools)

Seat belts are not compulsory and are absent from all but the most modern vehicles.

Random breath tests, but these are rarely carried out. The blood alcohol limit is 80mg/100ml.

Petrol comes in two grades: *especial* and *regular*. Both are leaded and as a rule only the dearer *especial* is avail-able to tourists. It is sold at 24-hour Servi-Cupet and Oro Negro petrol stations for dollars only. Locals use these stations (if they can afford to) or their own peso stations (which do not often have fuel). Regular petrol should not be used in hire cars: if it is, hire companies will charge heavily, as it blocks carburettors.

Havanautos have two 24-hour breakdown telephone numbers – ☎ 338176 or 338177. Try not to have an accident: foreigners tend to be held responsible for accidents unless they are some distance away from their legally parked vehicle.

PERSONAL SAFETY

Cuba is still the safest place in Latin America, but with the increase in tourism, the crime rate has risen. The most likely target is your hire car, but bag snatching in the street, especially during festivals, is also rising in frequency.

- avoid great shows of wealth
- carry your bag around your neck rather than on your shoulder
- avoid dimly lit streets at night.

Police assistance:
☎ **116** from any call box

There is an efficient police service, but officers are unlikely to speak English.

TELEPHONES

Cuba's telephone system is being updated, but can be a cause of frustration. Card phones (buy cards in hotels or photoservice shops), are now common in all major cities and can be used to direct dial abroad at $5.85 per minute. Phoning from a hotel will be expensive ($8 per minute). All major towns have a *centro telefónico* where you can borrow a booth. You are unlikely to be allowed to make a collect call, as Cuba wants to earn hard currency from your call. To make an international call from your hotel room add the prefix 88, and from a card phone add 119.

POST

Post Offices
Cuba has very few official mail boxes, so tourists are best advised to post their letters and postcards in a hotel or at the airport. Even so, mail delivery is erratic, with letters taking anything up to a month to reach Europe. Stamps are much cheaper at post offices, where they are sold for pesos, than at hotels, where you have to pay in dollars.

There is no *post restante* service, but your hotel will probably oblige.

ELECTRICITY

Cuba's power supply is 110v AC, 60Hz as in the US, though some of the newer hotels are now offering sockets at 220v as well. New, Spanish-built hotels often use European round-pin plugs instead of the American flat ones, but it can be hard to find this out in advance.

TIPS/GRATUITIES

Yes ✓ No ✗		
Restaurants	✓	5–10%
Cafeterias/fast-food outlets	✓	5–10%
Bars	✓	coins
Taxis	✓	round up bill
Porters	✓	$1
Chambermaids	✓	$1
Museum/tour guides	✓	coins
Hairdressers	✓	coins
Car park attendants	✓	$1
Musicians	✓	$1

PHOTOGRAPHY

What to photograph: wild country, idyllic beaches, interesting towns, rare birds and wonderfully photogenic people.

Restrictions: do not photograph military installations, soldiers, factories, airports, bridges on main roads, ports, radio and TV stations and shots from aircraft. If in doubt ask – it could save considerable heartache later.

Where to buy film: colour print film is usually available at hotels and in some of the larger towns, but it is best to take both your own film and camera batteries.

HEALTH

Insurance

Medical insurance is strongly recommended, though the cost of treatment is low in comparison to North America and Europe. Resorts and major cities have international clinics for tourists. Health services are excellent, arguably the best in Latin America, but lack of money often means medicines are not available. Note that visitors admitted to hospital are likely to be tested for HIV/AIDS and will be deported if found to be a carrier.

Dental Services

Dental care should be covered by your medical insurance. Check that it is before you set off, as you will have to pay for any treatment. The quality of dental services in Cuba is excellent.

Sun Advice

The biggest health risk in Cuba is from the sun – between May and September temperatures rise above 30°C. Apply plenty of sun cream, wear a hat and drink plenty of water, even on cloudy days. Bring your own sun cream, as it can be expensive or hard to find on the island, although bigger hotels and branches of Tangara now sell it.

Drugs

If you are on medication take adequate supplies with you as there will be no problem taking them into the country, whereas local supplies may be limited. Cuba has excellent pharmacies, and these operate a 24-hour rota. Local ones charge much lower prices than the ones in international clinics, but are usually also less well stocked.

Safe Water

The water supply in most upmarket hotels is excellent, but elsewhere tap water should be treated with caution. Bottled mineral water is recommended and is readily available.

CONCESSIONS

Be prepared to receive no concessions.

Students can take their cards, but are unlikely to receive anything but a shrug, as only those studying in Cuba are eligible for concessions.

Senior citizens There are no special concessions for the older visitor, but as museum entry and travel are very inexpensive, this should not present a problem.

CLOTHING SIZES

Most local clothing comes in 'try-it-and-see' sizes, but the dollar shops do offer sizing, usually based on the US system.

USA/Cuba	UK	Europe	
36	36	46	Suits
38	38	48	
40	40	50	
42	42	52	
44	44	54	
46	46	56	
8	7	41	Shoes
8.5	7.5	42	
9.5	8.5	43	
10.5	9.5	44	
11.5	10.5	45	
12	11	46	
14.5	14.5	37	Shirts
15	15	38	
15.5	15.5	39/40	
16	16	41	
16.5	16.5	42	
17	17	43	
6	8	34	Dresses
8	10	36	
10	12	38	
12	14	40	
14	16	42	
16	18	44	
6	4.5	37.5	Shoes
6.5	5	38	
7	5.5	38.5	
7.5	6	39	
8	6.5	40	
8.5	7	41	

- There is an airport tax, $25 (at time of writing), payable on all international flights.
- It is illegal to export Cuban pesos from the country (though, curiously, mint-condition notes are sold at the airports as a souvenir). It is allowable, but pointless, to export convertible pesos.
- It is recommended that those not travelling with a package tour arrive 2 hours before departure time.

LANGUAGE

Cubans speak Spanish, but with a number of 'Cubanisms' which owe their existence to the long years of isolation from Spain and the influence of the African slaves. The pronunciation is Latin American – that is, ce, ci and z are pronounced 's' not 'th' as in Castilian Spanish. However, Spanish speakers will have no difficulty in understanding or in being understood. Many young people also speak English.

🛏	hotel	*hotel*	reservation	*reserva*
	bed and breakfast	*dormir y desayunar*	with bath	*con baño*
			with shower	*con ducha*
	single room	*habitación sencilla*	with a view	*con vista*
			air-conditioned	*climatizado*
	double room	*habitación doble*	toilet	*servicio*
	one person	*una persona*	lift	*ascensor*
	one night	*una noche*	hot water	*agua caliente*
💱	bank	*banco*	commission charge	*comisión*
	exchange office	*cambio*	payment	*pago*
	post office	*correos*	foreign currency	*moneda extranjera*
	banknote	*billete*		
	coin	*moneda*	receipt	*recibo*
	travellers' cheque	*cheque de viajero*	hard currency	*divisa/moneda effectivo*
	credit card	*tarjetas de crédito*	Cuban currency	*moneda nacional (pesos)*
	money	*moneda/dinero*		
🍴	café	*café*	meat	*carne*
	bar	*bar*	fish	*pescado*
	breakfast	*desayunar*	dessert	*postres*
	lunch	*almuerzo*	bill	*cuenta*
	dinner	*cena*	beer	*cerveza*
	table	*mesa*	wine	*vino*
	waiter/waitress	*camerero/ camerera*	water	*agua*
			rum	*ron*
🚌	train	*tren*	boat	*barco*
	railway station	*estacíon/ terminal de tren*	ticket	*boleto*
			ticket office	*taquilla*
	airport	*aeropuerto*	timetable	*horario*
	flight	*vuelo*	car	*autocoche*
	bus	*ómnibus (gua-gua in 'Cuban')*	taxi	*taxi*
			bicycle	*bicicleta/ciclo*
💬	yes	*si*	do you speak English ?	*habla usted inglés ?*
	no	*no*		
	please	*por favor*	I don't understand	*no entiendo*
	thank you	*gracias*	where is... ?	*dónde está...?*
	hello	*hola*	open	*abierto*
	goodbye	*adiós*	closed	*cerrado*
	good morning	*buenas días*	today	*hoy*
	good afternoon	*buenas tardes*	tomorrow	*mañana*
	good night	*buenas noches*	ladies	*damas/ellas/ mujeres*
	excuse me	*perdón/permiso*		
	you're welcome	*de nada*	gentlemen	*caballeros/ ellos/hombres*
	how much ?	*cuánto*		

INDEX

Acknowledgements

The Automobile Assocation wishes to thank the following photographers, libraries and associations for their assistance in the preparation of this book:

EMILY HATCHWELL 122b; MAGNUM PHOTOS LTD 14b (R Burri); FRED MAWER 7b, 8b, 8c, 12/13, 17b, 19b, 26b, 58b, 60b, 61b, 64/5, 65b, 75b, 90b, 96b, 97b, 100b; MRI BANKERS' GUIDE TO FOREIGN CURRENCY 119; NATURE PHOTOGRAPHERS LTD 13b (E A Janes); RICHARD SALE 12b, 25b, 27b, 33b, 62, 71, 72a, 73a, 74a, 75a, 76a, 77a, 78, 79a, 80a, 81a, 83a, 117b; SPECTRUM COLOUR LIBRARY 16b; MIREILLE VAUTIER 11, 15a, 16a, 17a, 18a, 19a, 20a, 20b, 20/1, 21a, 22a, 23a, 24a, 25a, 26a, 74b, 74c; WORLD PICTURES LTD 5b, 15b, 55b, 59b

The remaining photographs were taken by Clive Sawyer and are in the Association's own picture library (AA PHOTO LIBRARY). Clive Sawyer would like to thank the following for their assistance and help in making this assignment one not to be forgotten: Christina Gibbons at Regent Holidays, Bristol; Carmen Mendez Acosta, representative for Havanatur; Hector del Valle Urizarri and his family in Old Havana; and John Lois, who guided him through Pinar del Río.

Author's Acknowledgements

Richard Sale would like to thank Gordon Burnett of Interchange, Croydon, and Abe Moore and Suzanne McManus of SuperClubs for all their help.

Revision management: Pam Stagg **Copy editor:** Audrey Horne **Page layout:** Jo Tapper
Researcher (3rd edition): CPA Media

Dear Essential Traveller

Your comments, opinions and recommendations are very important to us. So please help us to improve our travel guides by taking a few minutes to complete this simple questionnaire.

You do not need a stamp (unless posted outside the UK). If you do not want to cut this page from your guide, then photocopy it or write your answers on a plain sheet of paper.

Send to: **The Editor, AA World Travel Guides, FREEPOST SCE 4598, Basingstoke RG21 4GY.**

Your recommendations...

We always encourage readers' recommendations for restaurants, nightlife or shopping – if your recommendation is used in the next edition of the guide, we will send you a *FREE* AA *Essential* **Guide** of your choice. Please state below the establishment name, location and your reasons for recommending it.

_____

_____

_____

_____

Please send me **AA *Essential*** _____

(*see list of titles inside the front cover*)

About this guide...

Which title did you buy?
AA *Essential* _____
Where did you buy it? _____
When? m̲ m̲ / y̲ y̲

Why did you choose an AA *Essential* Guide? _____

_____

_____

_____

_____

Did this guide meet your expectations?
Exceeded ☐   Met all ☐   Met most ☐   Fell below ☐
Please give your reasons _____

_____

_____

_____

continued on next page...

Were there any aspects of this guide that you particularly liked? _____

_____

_____

_____

Is there anything we could have done better? _____

_____

_____

_____

_____

About you...

Name (*Mr/Mrs/Ms*) _____

Address _____

_____

_____ Postcode _____

Daytime tel nos _____

Which age group are you in?
Under 25 ☐ 25–34 ☐ 35–44 ☐ 45–54 ☐ 55–64 ☐ 65+ ☐

How many trips do you make a year?
Less than one ☐ One ☐ Two ☐ Three or more ☐

Are you an AA member? Yes ☐ No ☐

About your trip...

When did you book? m m / y y   When did you travel? m m / y y
How long did you stay? _____
Was it for business or leisure? _____
Did you buy any other travel guides for your trip?
If yes, which ones? _____

_____

Thank you for taking the time to complete this questionnaire. Please send
it to us as soon as possible, and remember, you do not need a stamp
(*unless posted outside the UK*).

Happy Holidays!